THE STUDENT MOVEMENT IN MANIPUR

THE STUDENT MOVEMENT IN MANIPUR

Ningthoukhongjam Urmila

AKANSHA PUBLISHING HOUSE
NEW DELHI - 110 002 (INDIA)

AKANSHA PUBLISHING HOUSE
4649/21-B, Ansari Road
Daryaganj, New Delhi - 110 002
Phones: 23263193, 9811582579
E-mail: ektabooks@yahoo.com

Student Movement in Manipur

First Published, 2007

ISBN 978-81-8370-141-9

PRINTED IN INDIA

Published by Akansha Publishing House, New Delhi - 110 002 and Printed at Capital Offset Press, Delhi

Dedicated to my mother

Angom Ningol Ningthoukhongjam Ongbi Chittamohini

who holds my hands when I need of and who shows the light at the end of every tunnel.

FOREWORD

It is a great pleasure for me to have gone through the book, *The Student Movement in Manipur,* written by Dr. N. Urmila, a young promising researcher and academician. People are talking a lot about the different type of contributions given by the student community in the developmental process of the society and state. When we look back to history we are able to come across many evidences where the students have played a pivotal role in the changing process of the given society. In a sense the student life can be treated as a symbol of justice, bravery and enthusiasm. During this period the students, by taking the role of pressure group, always put forward a lot of enthusiastic ideas and suggestions for the betterment of the society. Such type of radicalist attitude in a positive direction is the significant contribution of the student community to their respective society.

Manipur is also not lagging behind in such type of social movement. Just after the merger of Manipur into India the people had enjoyed an opportunity to witness the activities of the student community. Apart from their academic activities they also played a major role in the social and political life of the state. As a student of social movement I am fully convinced that any type of positive changes in the political and social life of any given society could be possible only when the younger generations are involved actively in a positive way. Such type of character was also very much prevalent in the case of Manipur. The participation of the students' community in the *'Statehood Movement'* of the *'State'* may be taken as a great contribution to the people. In addition to this their active participation against the large scale influx of foreign nationals also rendered a very significant contribution in the process of fostering promotion and maintenance of the traditional national character to the indigenous people of Manipur.

Here I am very happy to note that the author, with her analytical capabilities, have successfully analyzed the role of the All Manipur Student Union in more categorical way. She analyzed the whole activities of the student body within the framework of sociological approach. I always considered it as a very intelligent and mature approach. The student movement, in fact, is still an ongoing process. As mentioned above that without the participation of the students the progress of the society and state may not be able to go in a positive direction. While preparing this monograph, the author consulted all the important primary sources and information. Therefore I take it as an original research work.

I am quite sure that Dr. N. Urmila Devi will carry on her research and academic work in a more and more comprehensive way. I am convinced that the book will render a lot of contribution to the academic world of the state of Manipur and it will give a great help to the new generation of the state.

N. Joykumar Singh
Dean
School of Social Sciences
Manipur University, Imphal

ACKNOWLEDGEMENT

I would like to thank Professor Naorem Joykumar Singh who guided me in exploring the political actions of the students in Manipur. His advice, thoughtful suggestions, valuable help has always kept my line of enquiry in the right track. Without his critical examination, I would not have been able to complete the book.

I also like to express my heartfelt gratitude to Professor M. Jiten Singh, Head of Department of History, Manipur University and Professor Kshetrimayum Bimola Devi, Dean, School of Social Sciences, Manipur University for their advice at times of need.

I sincerely would like to acknowledge the warm cooperation of the following persons and some others whose names were missing in my diary: Professor Naorem Sanajaoba, Mr Leihaothabam Sarat Sharma, late Mr Nongmeikappam Sanajaoba, Dr Kh Loken, Mr Lairenjam Gojendra, Mr Narumbam Achouba, Dr Ningombam Basanta, Mr Khangembam Kuleshwar, Mr Meisnam Khelen, Mr S Noren. Mr Salam Ibohal, Mr Loitongbam Iboyaima, Mr Arunkumar (Boyai), Mr Yenkokpam Priyokumar, Mr S Sarat, Mr Raj Kumar Bobichand, Dr Laimayum Bishwanath Sharma, Mr A C Netrajit, Mr L C Somorendro, Mr Raj Kumar Tenedy. I am very sorry for those whose names could not be mentioned here. It is all my fault.

I also like to express my sincere gratitude to all the staff members of the Criminal Investigation Department, Government of Manipur for allowing me to go through the police records of the student activities during the period under study.

I also like to acknowledge Mr Irengbam Arun, Editor, *Ireibak* for his careful and critical examination when the book is about to print. His editing technique is really useful in shaping the book in the present form.

Lastly but not the least, I express my thanks to Dr K Ibo Singh, Department of Political Science, Manipur University under whom I started my work and who had spared his valuable time from 1991 to 1999 to supervise my work progress. I shall remain ever indebted to him for his help and support.

Ningthoukhongjam Urmila

CONTENTS

1
INTRODUCTION

I

The lexical meaning of 'Student' is usually given at two levels:

1. anyone who is learning a subject matter;
2. anyone who is enrolled in a formal educational institution.

Generally, the 'student' is taken as of the second meaning. But, there are various other connotations of the word, 'Student'. In many works on the history of social conflicts, contemporary social problems, the *Students* are not as simple as its lexical meaning.

To Alain Touraine[1], the students are a new force comparable to the labour class. He says, *If it is true that knowledge and technical progress are the motors of the new society, as the accumulation of capital was the motor of the preceding (industrial) society, does not the university then occupy the same place as the great capitalist enterprises formerly did? Thus, is not student movement, in principle, at least, of the same importance as the labour movement of the past?*

On the other hand, students are seen by some bureaucratic orthodoxy, as the 'traditional middle class'. To them, any separate student strategy or movement would merely reflect its petit-bourgeois provenance[2].

These views are over-generalized. While defining students, we should consider (a) the origin, (b) the situation, and (c) the social destination. These factors are related with the historical experience of a 'historical bloc' (in the Gramscian sense). As the origin and destination of the students are similar in the developing countries, the student situation is more important. Except for a few student bodies functioning as wings of political parties, majority of the individual students in Manipur are rebellious by nature to the existing political authority, although without a long term political goal. Considering such historical realities, we can safely say, in a sense, *students are not a class, but a temporary occupation: they are apprentice workers who no sooner become conscious of themselves as a community they tend to be dispersed - and hence neutralized* [3].

The students' role in the polity system emerged actively in the 19th century. The German student body of *Burschenschaft,* founded in 1815, sought to influence the government for liberalizing its machineries and for unifying the German states into one nation. It also aimed to eliminate the out-of-fashion medieval practices in the University so that an academic freedom in learning and teaching could be attained. Many student bodies came up in history with different aims and objects since then. Some of them were highly charged with political ideology; many other bodies acted as pressure groups or interest groups with or without a definite political ideology. *By the twentieth century the cumulative experience of generations of fighting students had produced a very high level of political consciousness in Latin American University students. It was they who succeeded in reforming their universities from 1918 onwards to a level which was unsurpassed during the following fifty years in America, Britain, France or Germany*[4]. It was the Cordoba Manifesto of 1918 that had charged the students actively to act with political interest in twentieth century political scenario of Latin America.

The Manifesto was the first declaration of student rights. It *denounced the old administration in which there was no reform of curricula, and no reform of rules, for fear that someone might lose his job because of the change and it announced: we want to eradicate from university organization the archaic and barbarous concept of authority which in university is a bulwark of absurd tyranny*[5]. The movement soon gained momentum to spread across the South American countries — in Peru they were made in 1919, Colombia in 1924, Paraguay in 1927, Brazil and Bolivia in 1928, Mexico in 1929 and Costa Rico in 1930s [6]. All these movements were but a legacy of active political involvement of the students in 19th century politics. *Latin American University youth played a leading part in the wars of independence at the beginning of the nineteenth century, and have gone on struggling against tyranny ever since*[7].

The students in United States have quite a different tradition. The first student union was established in 1896 at the University of Pennsylvania; but major unions came up only in 1930. *This growth is the result of general acceptance by educators of the concept that leisure-time activities have educational value - that much development of students takes place outside the classroom*[8]. In the 1960s, students started to demand and often get a much larger share in shaping policies than the Universities traditionally allowed them to. Notable *changes were evident in the scope of the student government. Nearly all US campuses have had for years some form of student government to help the administration maintain effective relations with the student body and to give students direct experience in self-government.*[9]

The most radical student group, Students for a Democratic Society (SDS) came into existence in 1960. Thomas E. Hyden, a student of the University of Michigan, published his famous **Port Huron Statement** in 1962; basing on the statement, SDS declared that *the American political system had failed to achieve social or international peace or end poverty and exploitation, and called for a* ***participatory democracy*** *in which individuals could share in social decisions that directly affected their lives*[10]. The SDS involved actively in Civil Rights movements at its initial stage; later, the group was in the forefront of the Anti-Vietnam War movement. It tried to mobilize the blacks, the poor, and the exploited to transform society by revolution and its ideology was direct confrontation with the American capitalist system.

In 1969, SDS split into three factions. The Progressive Labour faction, a pro-Mao group, tried to divert campus members of SDS away from Campus politics and into the working-class movement. The Revolutionary Youth Movement-II sought to transfer the University into an area of Revolutionary action. The Weatherman faction, also known as Revolutionary Youth Movement-I, considered itself the vanguard of violent revolution, with students, workers, and blacks presenting a united front. They endorsed terrorism as part of an armed struggle and conducted workshops on explosives and sabotage. At its 1972 convention SDS was clearly controlled by the Progressive Labour faction, doctrinaire and disciplined but opposed to violence [11].

Many countries of the third world produced various

militant student movements in the twentieth century. In Cuba (1958), Czechoslovakia (1968), China (1919) students played vital roles in changing the existing political order. In 1933, the students in Cuba *were mainly instrumental in bringing down the Machado dictatorship in alliance with a group of rebellious army sergeants; and under Batista's second dictatorship, in 1952-58, they played a leading role in both the urban and the rural resistance movements. In March 1957, they organized an unsuccessful assassination attempt on Batista and several of their leaders were killed; subsequently they participated in sabotage in Havana and many went to the mountains of Oriente to fight with the Rebel Army*[12]. Even after the Castro's revolution, the students participated in every sphere of state politics.

The China scene is more interesting in the sense that students' action preceded the Chinese Communist movement. The Peking University, founded in 1898, was the academic centre of the Chinese Revolution. The Peking students staged a gigantic demonstration on 4 May 1919 against Japanese imperialism, its expansion into Manchuria. *In the civil war between the Koumintang and the Chinese Communist Party, the majority of the students opted for Mao Tse-Tung and supported the Chinese Revolution of 1949* [13]*. Upto 1925, the students were more powerful than the Party itself. The first Party secretary, Chen Tu Hsiu, was a professor at Peking University. Mao Tse Tung himself was initiated into politics through student movements in Peking and Changsha, and one of his first political experience was a student strike in sympathy with 4 May movement, in June 1919*[14]. The students in China too took major roles in carrying out Mao's unique cultural revolution [15].

The Japanese experience is, however, slightly different from others. The Japanese students started to perform political actions in an organized way in 1960. They rallied against the renewal of the Security Treaty between Japan and US. There were a series of demonstrations over this issue. In addition, there were two equally important issues in 1960s. The three separate issues of the struggle were the resignation of Kishi for his action of 19 May, the cancellation of Eisenhower's visit, and the prevention of the Security Treaty[16]. But, there was tension between the different student bodies in Japan. The most serious conflict was between Private Universities and National Universities. At the ideological front, though All Japan Federation of Student Self Government Association swept Japan for about 20 years in post war period, Japanese students started to leave aside the Communist Party in 1955-56, In *1958, two new organizations were set up which were to exercise a great influence over the students - the Kakukyodo (which was a political organization) and the Shagakudo (which was a purely student body_... The JCP groups or* ***anti-mainstream*** *faction regarded the US as the main target; whereas the mainstream were more concerned with internal Japanese issues and the overthrow of the existing power structure* [17]. In spite of these conflicts, the student movement *has played a historic role in any world perspective. It pioneered mass revolutionary action in an industrialized country, years before it was achieved in Europe and America... it has demonstrated that students can forge effective links with the most oppressed classes in society - workers and peasants*[18].

Student movement in South-East Asia emerged out of the anti-colonial political movements. Though political consciousness of the students were shaped by the nationalist movements, the students in the region was not able to develop as a community. This is because of the fact that there were only a limited number of educational institutions. But they had been associated *with nascent political elements outside the University community. The students were articulated in discussion groups, youth congresses, women's congresses and in politically oriented articles published in a variety of newspapers and journals*[19].

In Burma, the students started taking part in political movements since the 1930s. The trouble was started by the announcement of Secretary Montagu in 1917-18. The Montagu-Chelmsfold *recommended that Burma's case should be reserved for special consideration, since her people were of a different race, having different problems. The storm of protest which suddenly arose in Burma when the nature of the alternative proposals for her political development became known took everybody by surprise. Burmese national sentiments flared up to a fever pitch*[20]. In the meantime, the opening of University of Rangoon in December, 1920 made room for a widespread student strike instigated by the politicians. *Discontent focused on the efforts of the British-appointed University governing agencies to stiffen preparatory standards and to free the University from political interference*[21]. But it was in 1930s, that the students could act for a movement of wider perspectives. By 1936 the Rangoon University Students Union (RUSU) became the headquarters of student agitation for the entire country. *The aggressive spirit of the student movement owed much to the frustration experienced by the vast majority of the students in their efforts to obtain diplomas and suitable employment... The sophisticated atmosphere of the University alienated many of Burma's youth from parental authority. The student movement was, therefore as much a product of an artificial and ill-adapted educational regimen as it was an expression of the rising tide of political disaffection. Many students developed a genuine interest in contemporary aspects of world affairs and in socialism, which were excluded from the curriculum*[22].

Another force which helped shape the student movement in Burma was the **Dobama Asiayone** (We Burmans Association). This Association was formed by amalgamating two national student organizations, the Dobama group and the All Burma Youth League in 1935. The members addressed each other as **Thakins** in youthful defiance of British rule and an affirmation of faith that Burmese were destined to be masters in their own country. The Thakins were, as a rule, dedicated nationalists, disdainful of fellow students who aspired for entry into the civil service and also hostile to middle classes politicians who mouthed nationalist slogans for enhancing their own political fortunes[23].

Though the memorable strike of February 1936 was led by the Rangoon University Student Union, it was precipitated by the Thakin leaders who had control of the RUSU. History tells that *The Thakin associates in the 1936 strike became the champions of Burmese nationalism against both the British and the Japanese, and they took over the political leadership of independent Burma after 1948* [24].

After the military seizure of power in 1955, RUSU and ABSU acted in alliance with the Burma Communist Party (BCP). Many Karen, Shan and Kachin students left the university to fight with their respective insurgent groups against Burmese Government. This was the beginning of the student action in free Burma [25].

In Indonesia, some students who had been educated in Holland became conscious of the disparity between colonized and free nations. In *the early 1920s, they consolidated their strength by transforming the existing Indonesian student organisation into a militant organization promoting unity and solidarity among people native to the Indonesian archipelago but stressing exclusiveness with respect to non-*

Indonesian students. This small but highly active student association, the ***Perhimpoenan Indonesia*** *(Indonesian association) was one of the first organizations to openly advocate an independent Indonesia* [26].

After the short drama of political powers in 1942-43 the Netherlands transferred sovereignty on 27 December, 1949. The political scenario of the independent Indonesia was dominated by a political confusion. *President Sukarno became in time an advocate of a centralized program of* ***guided democracy*** *in an endeavour to exploit the revolutionary fervour of Communist partisans, who also opposed particularism and multiparty rule. His* ***Pantja Sila*** *ideal included faith in Allah and devotion to nationality, humanity, democracy and social justice; but the precise meanings were unclear, and implementation was sadly lacking. Sukarno's attempt to bridge the chasm between Islam and communism incurred the inevitable-risk that he would alienate both sides and thus compromise the achievement of exposed objectives*[27]. His proposals were strongly objected to by the Muslim parties and thus started the chronic conflict between the Islamic and leftist groups. This had a strong impact on the student politics in 1960s.

The student politics in 1965 was dominated by the conflict between Islamic groups (especially HMI) and leftist groups (CGMI). *On October 25, 1965, a group of representatives from virtually all student associations (the major exceptions being CGMI and two other communist-oriented organizations) acted on the proposal of the Minister of Higher Education and Sciences and formed a new federative student organization. The new organization was called the Indonesian Students' Action Front or KAMI... The fate of KAMI assassinations carried out by the* ***30th of September movement*** *was revealed in the importance which students* *attached to the distinction between what they labelled the* ***older order*** *and the* ***new order*** *toward they were working. The three-fold demand of KAMI hinted at a broad reform orientation: (i) dissolution of the Indonesian Communist Party (ii) dismissal of cabinet members and formation of a new cabinet, (iii) reduction of prices*[28]. This was the starting point of a new beginning of student politics in post independence era of Indonesia.

Indian students entered politics, like many other colonized countries, with the emerging and growing nationalist movement. In *1928, a student organization was formed in Punjab under the leadership of Lala Lajpat Rai. In the same year, an All Bengal Students' Association was presided by Jawaharlal Nehru. In 1936 an All India Students' Federation was established... The Congress leaders, in 1945, established... All India Students' Congress, In 1950, this organization was dissolved*[29]. But after India got its sovereignty in 1947, student bodies were widely charged with different (even state-based) student organizations. Some notable national level bodies are All India Students' Federation, Students' Federation of India, National Students' Union of India, Akhil Bharatiya Vidhyarthi Parishad. Assessing the present student politics, as quoted in Babul Fadia[30], Philip G. Altbach says, *The student movement had lost its sense of militant unity and ideological purpose... The nationalist fervour of the pre-independance period has been replaced by generally unorganized and sporadic agitation usually aimed at specific grievances*. The four grievances are (a) demands upon non-university authorities on issues (b) Student demands by students upon universities on issues of special concern (c) sporadic, generally unorganized outburst by students only vaguely associated with concerned demands, (d) activities associated with larger political movements in the areas surrounding the school, college or university.

There are many student organisations operating in Indian states, charged with regionalism or regional oriented ideology. For example, the student politics started in Assam was in nationalistic line during the colonial period. The pre-independent student organizations were affiliated to political parties. But, after independence, *a feeling was developed among the students to organize students more on no-party line. The Assam Students' Association which came into existence in September 1959 was organized on non-partisan, non-political and democratic foundation. It came to stand by the larger and collective interests of the students of Assam as well as to solve the problems common to the students of Assam as well as to promote the spirit of culture, literature, sports etc... (But) because of its participation in Refinery movement and Language movement it was branded as partisan and politically motivated. Therefore, there was mounting pressure for the organization of a student union whereby the students of all classes irrespective of language, religion, hills or plains could take a common platform*[31]. After this, a new student organization, All Assam Students' Union, came into being in 1967 with a different political colour.

Like other states of India, Manipur students have been engaging in their own political action. But, unlike many others, the student politics in Manipur did not originate from the nationalist or independence struggle. It was only in post-independence period that some political parties like the Manipur Pradesh Congress and the Socialist Party tried to rally the students in their party activities. But, during the mid-60s with the formation of All Manipur students' Union, the state witnessed a new turn in student politics. The history of the All Manipur Students' Union (AMSU) reflects not only the different activities of youth and students in the state, but also, the changing political ideas which have penetrated the collective mind and the psyche of the student community.

REFERENCES

1. "Naissance d'un Mouvement Etudian" in Le Monde, 7 & 8 March 1968
2. see Alexander Cockburn and Robin Blackburn, *Student Power,* Penguin, London
3. Alexander Cockburn & Robin Cockburn, op.cit., pp.35-36
4. George Paloczi-Horath, *Youth Up In Arms,* Weidenfeld and Nicolson, London, 1971:184
5. Alexander Cockburn and Robin Blackburn, *Student Power,* Penguin, London, 1969:288-289
6. Fred Halliday, "Students of the World Unite", *ibid.*:289
7. George Paloczi-Horath, *op. cit.*:183
8. *Encyclopedia Americana*, Vol.7: 255
9. *ibid.:* 254
10. *ibid.:* Vol. 25: 809
11. *ibid.*
12. George-Paloczi, op. cit.: 293
13. "Student Movement" in *Lexicon Universal Enclyclopedia,* Vol.18: 307
14. Fred Halliday in A. Cockburn and R. Blackburn, *Op.cit.*:299
15. see "Chinese Communist Youth League" in *China Quartery,* No.12, Oct-Dec, 1962
16. see Fred Halliday, *op.cit.*:296-7
17. *ibid.:* 295-6
18. *ibid.:* 298
19. Stephen A Douglas and Harsja Bachtiar, "Indonesian Students:

Generation of 1966" in Philip G Altbach, *The Student Revolution: a Global Analysis,* Lalvani, Bombay, 1970: 158

20. D G E Hall, *A History of South East Asia,* McMillan, London, 1968:740
21. John F Cady, *South East Asia: Its Historical Development,* Tata McGraw Hill, New Delhi, 1976:509
22. *ibid.:* 521
23. *ibid.*
24. *ibid.:* 522
25. see Joself Silverstein, "Burmese Student Politics in a Changing Society" in Philip G Altbach, *op.cit.*
26. Stephen A Douglas, *et. al., op.cit.:* 158
27. John F Cady, *op. cit.,* see also, D G E Hall, *op.cit.:* 893-9
28. Stephen A Douglas, *et. al., op.cit.:* 161
29. Babulal Fadia, *Pressure Groups in Indian Politics,* Radiant, New Delhi, 1980: 61
30. *ibid.:* 61-62
31. Indrani Barua, *Pressure Groups in Assam,* Omsons, New Delhi, 1990: 20

2

EMERGENCE OF THE STUDENTS' APEX BODY

I

THE NATURE OF AMSU

The All Manipur Students' Union (AMSU) was born in the aftermath of an incident in which police fired upon agitating students on 27 August 1965 at the Chief Commissioner's compound of Imphal. Four persons including three students died in the incident. The students were demanding price control of rice and introduction of ration cards in the public distribution system.

The AMSU is a student body having neither a specific political ideology nor a specific political responsibility in the society. Like many other student bodies in India, it is committed to act politically, whenever it feels necessary, in the interests of Manipur, Manipuri society and the student community. No one is certain of the relationship between the elite groups and the AMSU *vis-a-vis* its political interest and manifest actions. But there is a cybernetic relation, it seems, between the AMSU decision-making process and the general political interest of the elite groups which is anti-establishment in nature. A closer examination is needed, however, to conclude in a positive manner. As the student community comprises more than half of the youth population, AMSU is the only body which could champion the cause of the common people's interest.

By the nature of its organizational setup, AMSU is not the student wing of any political party. It acts, in the existing socio-political environment, as a pressure group. Again, it has no particular political interest from which it would evaluate any issue or determine its political demands. The political interest of AMSU lies in the social system, as and when determined by its elected Executive Council. Here, theoretically speaking, a political fact may be percieved differently by two different Executive Councils of AMSU as there may be no common political interest between the two Councils.

According to **Encyclopedia Britanica**[1], *An interest group is a number of people with a deep and continuing interest in a particular issue, who evaluate other current issues on the basis of their implications for this central interest.* Gabriel A. Almond et.al. are of the opinion that an interest group is *a set of individuals who are aware of these shared interests. The interest group may reflect only their occasional involvement*[2]. In this line of thinking, an interest group is a group having a more or less permanent shared interest. AMSU, theoretically, has no such permanent interest except the **aims and objects** embodied in its Constitution. The materialization of the aims and objects are not directed by a permanent ideological sanction or political interest. But, in praxis, AMSU develops a sort of interests which is linked with the **pride and growth** of Manipuri society. Hence, AMSU can be considered as a political body, when it carries out political action, and as a quasi-interest group having diffused responsibility and diffused power. In other words, AMSU is a non-institutional interest group that articulate political interest from the commonly perceived interests in the larger social system. Non-institutional interest group is one, that is not a specialized organization, but that has a relatively continuous interest over time.

With the articulated interest, AMSU, in its role in the political system of the State, acts as a pressure group. As a body AMSU may, not doubt, have certain political interests at a particular point of time that do not need any governmental action to attain the desired goal. But, at large, AMSU acts as a pressure group to influence the governmental decision making process with demands or to alter the existing politics and programmes so that particular interest(s) may be materialized. Unlike other permanent pressure groups, AMSU cannot pursue the government with long term demands. Here we can use the definition given by Dack C.Plano and Milton Greenberg in their **The American Political Dictionary:** *An organized interest group in which members share common views and objectives and actively carry on programmes to influence government officials and policies.* While taking AMSU as pressure group, we consider the praxis attributes of the body.

The political demands of a pressure group are overt political action; many political actions are not necessarily manifested in public. When the activities are not related with the business of the government, AMSU organizes seminars and conferences etc. to find a way of attaining certain political goals. The body puts forward demands only when the goal involves governmental action. One would say **when AMSU disagrees with a decision taken by the state, it will bring up a demand; when it agrees, it does not act overtly.** So, the demands are, by and large, originated from public frustration out of the existing political system. The major political demands in last 27 years are the Statehood, Secularization of educational institutions, inclusion of Manipuri language in Schedule VIII of the Indian Constitution, and the Foreigners' Issue. These demands are socially accepted and culturally sanctioned.

The All Manipur Students' Union always keep in mind the national pride and the societel interest while visualising its demands. The demand of price-control and the conversion of private colleges into government colleges etc. can also be seen in many of the AMSU resolutions. But demands of such nature have little value in the society. Whereas, cultural recognition and overwhelming societel response could be seen in the case of the Foreigners' issue, the Language issue, and the demand for repeal of the Armed Forces Special Powers (Assam and Manipur) Act, 1958. Because, these issues could strike at the core of the collective sentiment of the society.The revivalist attitude of certain elite groups play a vital role in popular acceptance of the demands. The use of words like **Kangleipak** and newly coined words in some leaflets circulated by AMSU, indicate such a tendency. **Kangleipak** is the proposed name of the state by certain sections of the population against the present Sanskrit name of **Manipur**. But other names are also proposed by many other groups.

Many a times, the political attitude of AMSU is shaped by the spirit of regionalism in the society. AMSU is, on many issues, often caught in a dilemma between the pro-constitutionalist and anti-constitutionalist poles. The **public image** of the state government as being inefficient, corrupt and untrustworthy leads to general disillusion and an anti-establishment attitude among the youth and the general population. It also provokes political action from AMSU and in its endeavour to **correct** the faults in the system, an anti-establishment attitude automatically seeps in. It again leads to use of violence in their agitations which in turn becoming a norm notwithsatnding the nature of the demands. Another manifestation of this ambivalent attitude is observed in the frequent boycott of the Republic Day Celebrations on 26 January. Such attitudes are also observed in the actions of other political groups in the state. But, such political action does not necesarily find a reflection in electoral politics. For instance, an anti-congress attitude does not affect the return of Congress M.L.As. in the state elections.

Birth of AMSU

There were student unions prior to 27 August, 1965. But those were mainly student wings of the political parties active in the state. As such, there was no apolitical forum of the students acting in the general interest of the students. The need of such a student forum was felt by some student leaders after the police firing on 27 August 1965, which left four persons dead and several others injured. Many student leaders were rounded up by the police in the aftermath of the incident and kept in jail.

On 27 August 1965, there was a mammoth procession of thousands of students demanding adequate availability of rice in the market and introduction of ration cards in the public distribution system. They had come to meet the then Chief Commissioner in his official bungalow. In fact, it was a continuation of several other processions staged during the last 10 days in Imphal. The first procession was on 18 August and it was mainly by the womenfolk, a replica of the **Nupi Lan of 1939** (a historic agitation of Manipuri women against the rice export policy of colonial British rulers). Their main demand was that, rice should be made available and sold to representatives of each and every family against ration cards alone, which should be introduced quickly and that the number of rice shops should be increased[3].

On the 27 August at 7 a.m., several people including some political leaders met the Chief Minister. During the discussion, the Chief Minister explained that the Government had already taken a decision on 23 August to introduce ration card system within 24 hours. At about 9.30 a.m. another group of about 300 persons had gathered at the Chief Commissioner's Bungalow. The Chief Commissioner accompanied by the Chief Minister had earlier gone to Kangchup, a village west of Imphal, to inaugurate a water supply system there. But the crowd waited till their return. They were able to meet the Chief Commissioner, the Chief Minister, and the Development Minister there at about 10.30 a.m. The crowd forcibly took away the Chief Commissioner to the nearby Johnstone School complex. While addressing the crowd, the Chief Commissioner explained that the food policy so far followed by the government had proved unsatisfactory. It was therefore decided to discard the old system and introduce ration cards within 48 hours from the date of submission of application. Cards would be issued through fair price shops, consumer shops, Panchayets and Panchayet Samities[4]. The crowd consisted of mainly grown-ups and elderly women in Chief Commissioner's bungalow. But on the highway, east of Johnstone School, a meeting consisting of women, young school and college students was also held.

At about 1 p.m. students from various schools and colleges organized a meeting at the Bir Tikendrajit Park. After the meeting at 2 pm, they proceeded towards the Chief Commissioner's Bungalow. They submitted a memorandum which demanded among others, exemption of school fees for the students during the scarcity period; increase in the number of fair price shops and the supply of food grains to the shops; and seizure of rice and paddy from hoarders [5]. At about 3 pm, the demonstrators started lambasting the government with loudspeakers and there was a tussle after that. The students wanted Chief Commissioner's written assurance, which was bluntly denied. At about 3.30 p.m. the police began lathi-charge and started firing tear gas shells to disperse the crowd. In response, some students started pelting stones at the bungalow and nearby vehicles.

By 3.40 pm, the riflemen started firing directly among the crowd. A student named O. Nabakumar (aged 20) instantly died of bullet injuries in the Chief Commissioner's compound. A driver of All India Radio, Imphal named Waikhom Nilamani Singh was dragged down from the jeep (Regd. No. J & K 5790) and bayoneted by a rifleman. The AIR jeep was coming towards the Chief Commissioner's Bungalow. He died on the way to the hospital. A bullet hit the left hand of one L. Mangi Singh. Another two students, Laishram Chaobhal (19) and Nameirakpam Pramodini sustained fatal injuries in the lathi charge. Altogether nine civilians excluding Government servants were admitted to the Civil Hospital, Imphal. Of these, four women namely S. Angoubi Devi, K. Loitang Devi, Tombi Devi and T. Bimola Devi were admitted to the female surgical ward. Five persons namely H. Ibohal Singh, Kalachand Singh, Maipaksana Singh, N. Budhi Singh and L. Mangi Singh[6] were admitted to the male surgical ward of the Civil Hospital.

The four persons who succumbed to their injuries in the 27 August 1965 incident were Oinam Nabakumar, Laishram Chaobhal, Nameirakpam Pramodini and Waikhom Nilamani.

Oinam Nabakumar born 19 May 1945 was a resident of Sega Road Thouda Bhabok Leikai, Imphal. After passing Matriculate Examination, he was studying Pre-University (Science) course at the D.M. College of Imphal. He was admitted to the course in 1964. Seven months prior to his death on 27 August 1965, he had married one Tongbram Nungshi who bore him a son on 7 October 1965. He was subsequently named Sahidchandra.

Laishram Chaobhal, born 1 June 1947, was a resident of Khurai Ningthoubung Leikai, Imphal. He was studying class X in Lamphel High School when the incident occurred. He sustained serious injuries in the police Lathi charge of 27 August 1965 and ultimately succumbed to his injuries on 22 September 1965.

Nameirakpam Pramodini, born 1st February 1946, was a resident of Singjamei Thongam Leikai, Imphal. She was a BA student of Manipur College, Imphal when the incident occurred.

Waikhom Nilamani, born 1 December 1937, was a resident of Ningthoujam Leikai. He was a driver of All India Radio, Imphal at the time of his death on 27 August 1965. He had just fathered a daughter on 5 August 1965. His wife was one Khangembam Thambalngangbi Devi.

The day after on 28 August 1965, a group of student activists organised a meeting at 8 a.m. at the residence of Leihaothabam Saratchandra of Keishampat. Nameirakpam Madhusudan Singh, a student of D.M. College, was in the chair. The meeting adopted several resolutions which included demands like, (1) Availability of sufficient quantity of rice to the public; (2) A judicial inquiry on the police firing of 27 August 1965; (3) Due compensation should for the victims of the incident; (4) Unconditional release of all the students arrested on 27 August. The most important resolution of the day was the proposal for formation of a student body at the state level, to press the above demands.

On 29 August, a second meeting was held at Uripok Tourangbam Leikai, Imphal at the residence of one Gurumayum Jatishwar with one N. Birendrakumar in the chair. In the meeting, the proposed student body was named as the **All Manipur Students' Union (AMSU).** An Executive Body was constituted with 36 representatives from different schools and colleges. The meeting selected Th. Gambhir and L. Tombi respectively as the President and General Secretary. Twenty-one persons were selected as Joint Secretaries who were again divided into Seven groups. The persons were N. Birendrakumar, H. Joy, M. Manikumar (first group); Y. Brojen, Pukhrambam Kullachandra, Seram Mangi (second group); L. Ibohal, Y. Dijen, Ng. Shankar (third group); L. Sharatchandra, Shyamkumar, S. Mangi (fourth group); Loitongbam Kanhai, K. Damudor Sarma, R.K. Laksana (fifth group); Kshetrimayum Tiken, P. Ibohal, Khwairakpam Subhas (sixth group); and N. Sarat, Kshetrimayum Nabakumar, G. Yaima (seventh group).

The Executive Council was, however, reconstituted at a meeting held on 12 September 1965 at Manipur Dramatic Union Hall, Imphal, after the release of seventeen student leaders who were arrested in connection with the 27 August agitation. All of them attended the meeting and a new Executive Council were constituted after dissolving the Body formed on 29 August. No formal elections were held, as a proper constitution was yet to be adopted then. Important offices such as the President and the General Secretary were given to the student leaders who were in jail[7]. Sanajaoba Naoriya (General Secretary, D.M. College Students' Union),

Thiyam Gambhir (General Secretary, Imphal College Students' Union), G. Joykumar Sharma(Ex-Editor, D.M. College Students' Union), Loitongbam Iboyaima (Ex Finance Secretary, Imphal College Students' Union) and Meinam Manikumar (a student of D.M. College) were respectively selected as President, Vice President, General Secretary, Finance Secretary and Publicity Secretary of the new Executive Council, besides 14 Executive Council members. An Advisory Body of 4 members and a Civil Defence Board of 5 members were also formed to assist the Executive Council. The Advisory Board was headed by N. Ibohal as Chairman and the Defence Board by Saikhom Mangi.

A Constitution Drafting Committee was formed in a meeting held on 10 February 1966 at the premises of All Manipur Boy's Scout Union, Singjamei with Sanajaoba Naoriya in the Chair. The Committee consisted of 7 members, namely, Th. Gambhir, Y. Rajendra, A. Birendra, Kh. Joysakhi, Jadumani, N. Ibohal and Kshetrimayum Iboyaima. The Draft Constitution was passed on 26 December, 1966 in the 20th sitting of the Executive Council at Wangkhei Paradise Club, Imphal. The first AMSU elections were held on 1st January 1967 under the said Constitution. This marked the formal birth of the **All Manipur Students' Union**: a new symbol of student unity and solidarity in the state.

AMSU in the total political system

The student community in Manipur became a more or less socio-political group, in late 1950's. This community, in spite of its class or political background, acts as a homogeneous body bound together by a sense of belongingness to the motherland. However, group behaviour was not influenced by the class background of the individual student in a significant way. In this context, we can consider

Seymour M. Lipset's view that "*Academic ecology, the social environment in which a student happens to find himself by virtue of his choice of University or academic field, tends to be more important than the class background in affecting his opinions.... Minority - majority social status also seems more important than the class background in affecting student propensity for action*"[8]. The role of academic ecology and that of class background is practically impossible because both of them are less differentiated in the social system of Manipuri society. The student composition in high and higher secondary schools, and colleges is more or less same. Further investigation may be made on the political behaviour of private school and college students. In the private schools, the students are mostly from the **privileged class** while students from **ordinary families** go to the government schools. On the other hand, the class background of the student in private colleges is relatively lower than that of leading three government colleges -D.M. College of Science, D.M. College of Arts and Commerce, G.P. Women's College; all of Imphal. The majority-minority aspect, too, subject to further investigation, had no obvious impact on the student politics. But some political differences were observed between the tribal and the Meitei (non-tribal) students over certain specific issues. The **Pangal** (non-tribal Muslim) students did not play a remarkable role as the number of students in high and higher secondary and colleges was very low.

The difference in political behaviour, political response to student actions among the students was visible remarkably at the topographical axis. The district-wise or locality-wise observations of the political behaviour will reveal such a difference. The proximity of a place to Imphal, the transport and media facilities and other geographical variations affect student's participation in a issue. This may be due to the fact that the centre of student politics in Manipur was Imphal.

The students' community which acts independently of many socio-economic variations, however, cannot take up long term political action plans. Many demands, even issues, are generally short term ones. The agitation periods are also short in time. This disability of long term action is because of the time-bound student career and the short span of higher education. The short academic life *makes the existence of on-going organizations and sustained leadership almost impossible. This problem is further aggravated by the fact that student participation in a movement is sporadic, for extra-curricular activity becomes difficult to pursue when the pressure of examinations grows intense, or when official disapproval is manifested* [9]. It can be noted here that some issues can drag the students to extended agitations. Such issues usually are emotionally charged. The longest agitation in Manipur was, however, that of the Foreigners' issue in 1980-81. The Foreigners' issue found political sanction as it was percieved as a **struggle for survival** of the society.

Thus, the student composition and its characteristic political actions demanded a new type of leadership. The traditional concepts of leadership cannot hold the community in order. A student leader is not necessarily an elected President; he is not a charismatic leader nor an organized vanguard. As the student body is not in the cadre-based structure, the leader is not born out of a hierarchically arranged order. The *new type of young politician regards himself as one of many, always replaceable, and he is regarded as such by his followers. If he speaks, he does not voice his own unique opinions as an individual, but rather speaks as the mouthpiece of his fellow students*[10]. The role of leadership in student politics may be further studied as to reveal the decision making process and to sort out the demands and/or supports in an existing system.

In an abstract system of polity, a student organization may be taken as a participant unit whose function is usually performed as a pressure group. The student body has a cybernetic relation with other units in power and responsibility, some student organizations may not be inclined to **support** any government; or they would simply remain silent on some issues which is not an unwanted one. So, they are often taken as an **agitating** body. In other words, they will supply the system with demand inputs, not in support. Among *inputs of a political system there are two basic kinds: demand and support. These inputs give a political system its dynamic character. They furnish it both with the raw material or information that the system is called upon to process and with the energy to keep it going* [11]. The student body while sharing only the demand input is specially taken as the **mouthpiece of the mass** against the **undemocratic** democracy. So the mass support to AMSU agitation is sustained even to its low-profile activities.

AMSU is not the lone student body; there are other student organizations like AISF, SFI, NSUI operating in the state. As the later groups are affiliated to political parties and committed to their respective political ideologies, they seldom represent public opinion and aspirations of the student community. In the political system, these bodies play a passive role of **criticizing and commenting** on particular and specific issues. But, AMSU as an active body, tries to create political situations in which the demands would transform into issues and then prepare the ground for launching movements. The body is, however, in a practical sense, an agitating body in the political system. This fact, thus, evolves a unique relationship between AMSU and the government. Functionally, the relation is of diffused type. This type *is one that is more or less vaguely defined and delimited* [12]. The AMSU-Government relationship is defined only when a particular situation is evolved out of the unique whole of diffused power and diffused responsibility in the larger power and responsibility structure.

At another axis of the relationship. AMSU units in the socio-political environment are interacting in universal and neutral terms. Theoretically, the environmental information are processed and decisions are taken by Executive Council of AMSU. But groups like the Pan Manipuri Youth League, Insurgent groups, Meitei revivalists, no doubt, play vital roles in information flow to AMSU directly or indirectly. The decision taken is independent of the information units. The demands put forward by AMSU, are thus, functionally related with the socio-political environments through these units. The demands are shaped by the environment; but *not all demands originate or have their major locus in the environment. Important types stem from situations occurring within a political system itself*[13]. Among the major demands of AMSU inclusive of such **inputs** are less in number. This is because of the nature of AMSU which is characterized by its interests in societal **power and prestige**. The demands have direct or indirect link with the axiological and survival crises in the state. They are seldom nor-oriented. The difference between nor-oriented and value-oriented action is very thin. The former is concerned with specific goals and is more likely a product of an emotional response to a specific limited issue. But the value-oriented one has broader ideological issues and when it is usually linked directly to a broader concern[14].

Demands are not equally weighed by the society as well as by the government. In Easton's words, *The occurrence of a demand, whether internal or external, does not thereby automatically convert it into a political issue. Many demands die at birth or linger on with the support of an insignificant fraction of the decision. Others become issues, an issue being a demand that the members of a political system are prepared to deal with as a significant item for discussion through the reorganized channels in the system*[15]. Thus, the main areas to be looked at while observing political actions of AMSU are the demands and their failure or success in the process of transformation into issues, the nature of the movements launched by this body.

AMSU, after agitation of a considerable period, usually sit with the government for negotiations. Many agreements or otherwise cannot give any significant direct output. This may due to inability of the negotiator to convince the government or lack of political determination in implementing the agreements on the part of the government. Thus a number of agreements or otherwise vanish as wastepaper in the **bureaucratic dustbin**. The student action often cannot toughen the representatives of AMSU and the government. Or it may be sign of politicians' failure to handle the bureaucratic officers.

No doubt, some of the agreements are not implemented because of the terms of agreement themselves. The main reason of such a situation is lack of skill on the part of the negotiator representing AMSU. Here we can say, all good agitators are not good negotiators. Distinguishing the two, Harold Lasswell notes, *The essential mark of the agitator is the high value which he places on the emotional response of the public. Whether he attacks or defends social institutions is a secondary matter... The agitator easily infers that he* *who opposes show bad faith or timidity. Agitators are notoriously contentions and undisciplined; many reforming ships are manned by mutineers. The agitator is willing to subordinate personal considerations to the superior claims of principle... The agitator sees **unworthy** motives there where others see the just claims of friendship...(He) trusts in mass appeals and general principles... live(s) to shout and write...(Agitators) conjoin away obstacles with the ritualistic repetition of principles. They become frustrated and confused in the tangled mass of technical detail upon which successful administration depends... They glorify men of outspoken zeal, men who harry the dragons and stir the public conscience by exhortation, reiteration and viterperation*[16].

To it, Robert A Dahl adds *By contrast, the negotiator is compromiser. If the agitator feels contempt for **unprincipled** conduct of the negotiator, the negotiator is baffled by the intrasigence of the agitator, who sacrifices immediate gains for abstract principles. The negotiator is more concerned with an acceptable solution to a conflict than a just or perfect solution*[17]. The main trouble of the negotiators of AMSU is the internal conflict between the merits of issue and time consumption of agitations. This inherent weakness of a student body becomes the soft target of the government.

Knowing the weakness, the government takes its own time for implementation of any agreement or so. AMSU has no pressure in the circle except casual personal contact. Moreover, any second agitation for implementation is always ineffective as the number of supporters decreases.

A few outputs given out after implementation are of regulation and symbolic types. There are four types of outputs: (a) Extractions (b) Regulation, (c) Distribution and (d) Symbols[18]. The regulation of human behaviour is related with the set of regulatory activities such as crime and punishment, enforcing duties and obligation. While the symbolic outputs include affirmation of values, displays of political symbols and statements of policies and intents.

II

Students play an important role in shaping the course of history in our country and other developing countries. Being educated and easily available in larger groups, they can be organised more easily than the general masses. At the same time, they easily respond to the calls given by the politically conscious leaders. Moreover, the student life is a stage in which they are trained for future leadership. Many well known political leaders were formerly student activists. This is true in many societies and countries. In this respect, Manipur cannot be an exception.

While tracing the history of student's movement in Manipur we are naturally drawn to the evolution of modern education. For, educational institutions are the centres of their activities.

Manipur received modern education the British Indian way much later than the rest of India. When the first three Universities were established in Bombay, Calcutta and Madras, Manipur had just established a high school. It was only in the first half of the twentieth century that high schools came into being in Manipur. The number of such institutions was limited. There was no facility even to go out of the state to appear in the matriculation examinations. Interestingly the first master's degree holder is still alive, while many of the first graduates are still alive though some of them are no more.

It is no wonder that, the youth went outside the state to receive higher education at the nearest centres of learning. Most of them went to Guwahati, Calcutta, Dacca, Syhlet etc. Though they went to these places in the hope of receiving higher education, it in no wonder that they were largely influenced by two things (I) western political ideals, institutions and practices and (ii) ongoing freedom struggle in the country i.e. India. Considering the first ones, they became aware of democratic ideals like liberty, equality fraternity, democratic institutions and practices like parliament, election of peoples representations etc. Nonetheless, some of them also were impressed by leftist ideology e.g. Socialists and Marxist ideologies. At the same time the ongoing movement - Swadeshi movement, non-cooperation movement, Quit India movement etc. impressed them. These students who witnessed these movements were inspired by the tactics and strategy adopted by Gandhi and other leaders of the Indian National Congress. They were also politically aroused when Gandhi made his clarion call to the nation during the Quit India Movement in which he emphasised the importance of the role to be played by the educated youth. Gandhi even hoped that the leadership in the said context should come from the students who were more informed and enlightened than their elders who were less educated or illiterate. He cited the Chinese instance in which the educated youth were in the forefront of all reform movements. Gandhi's views was widely accepted and appreciated. His strategy to involve the students in the freedom struggle was considered to be correct and timely. It was not considered to be an attempt to wean them away from their schools and colleges aimlessly. They were rather inspired to lead the country to freedom. "When your house is on fire nothing can be more urgent than saving the house", he said.

Inspired and influenced by the strategy and tactics adopted by the Indian National Congress under Gandhi; and also supplemented by western democratic ideals, principles and practices, the young educated Manipuris started various socio-religious movements during the period (1918-1939). The protest against foreign goods was of political significance. Movement against monarchy and colonialism was another political activity. It is not possible to incorporate all those movements in this limited space. But all these socio-religious and political movements were spearheaded by the educated youths.

Apart from socio-religious and political movements there were other activities well connected with literary activities. Though, many of these educated ones either became politicians or government employees, other sections were involved in organising literary activities like debates, recitations, establishment of libraries, clubs, scout movements etc. However, these activities were interrupted by the outbreak of the Second World War.

The end of the Second World War in 1945 leading to the reopening of schools all over the state following restoration of normal civil life brought with it a new political awakening among the students in the state. Students studying outside Manipur particularly in Gauhati, Shylet now in Bangladesh, Calcutta and such other prominent cities had their own unions engaged in extracurricular activities. They brought with them the new trend in Manipur under the students studying in the schools and the newly started Dhanamanjuri College (1946) responded with enthusiasm. Formation of the students union in the institutions began from the year 1946-47. The D.M. College Students' Union became a model by itself. The leading High Schools like the Johnstone, the Churachand, the Ram Lal Paul and the Tombisana had soon started having students' unions one after another. The activities of the union had much wider social impact. Debating competitions became a very regular activity sponsored by one or the other union. The student activities during the period 1946 to 1956 besides their academic and extracurricular activities were critical against the establishment in general. The concept of the ruling party was not born then in the state. In 1946-47, the political situation was peculiar. Independence was attained on the 15 August, 1947.

Nevertheless, during the pre-Independence period the student activities were there with a political implication. Student meeting the Maharaja and the relevant members of the Manipur State Darbar to present their demand for printing of text books and improvement of school facilities were frequent. After Independence, the activities of the students wing of the political parties were considered the activities of their parent organisation. The regime of the elected assembly 1948 to 1949 saw student activity mostly against the government. The then ruling party known as the Praja Shanti did not have a student wing. The student organisations including the Congress wing were active against the then government. Manipur's merger with the Indian Union brought a spell of undemocratic government upto 1957. From 1957 to 1963 there was a spell of six years which saw Manipur split into two administrations namely the Chief Commissioner's Government and the Union Territory administration run by the representatives of the people. During this period also, student activity were mostly against the establishment. The Dhanamanjuri College students strike in 1951 became a state wide movement which rocked the administration. Students irrespective of their political affiliation joined the strike which demanded the removal of the Principal who ultimately had to leave the college when the administration followed up the assurance given to the striking students.

At the state level, a students' organisation known as the All Manipur Students' Federation came into being in 1946. The organisation was represented by students belonging to various political parties - Congress, Communists and Socialists. On 30 October 1946, the body organised a conference at Churachand High School. The basic objective of the conference was to work for the "Unity of students, community of Meiteis, Muslim and of the Hills". The Federation organized five conferences. Such conferences became the beginning of students movement in Manipur. They demanded (1) Establishment of responsible government in Manipur; (2) Development of Imphal City and rural municipalities; (3) Free primary education system; (4) Establishment of new schools and colleges; (5) Proper facilities for students; (6) Combined administration of the hill people and the valley people; (7) Human rights.

The aforesaid students' federation could be regarded as the starting point of students' political activities. For about two years the organisation provided a democratic forum for future politicians, some of them are still active in the political arena both at the state and national levels. However, this forum did not survive in its original form. The Congress and the Socialists were separated from the federation which was left to communists. The Congress wing came to the known as Students' Congress. After one year the Students' Congress was split. The Socialists formed their own organisation - Young Socialist League. The then ruling party Praja Shanti did not have a students' wing. Almost all the activities of the students were controlled by the Congress, Communists and the Socialists. Penetration of the socialists elements in the students community was significantly successful.

The period upto the formation of the All Manipur Students Union (AMSU) (1965) is a period in which socialist elements were very active. As the Congress party was the ruling party, student activists of the party had to struggle to make political impact on the society. During this period the Socialist elements controlled the Students' Union of the D.M. College. Communist supporters among students were also there but were less widespread with a sprinkling here and there in the state-wide student movement. They tried to contribute their share in the political awakening of the State. Now, it would be worthwhile to the circumstances which led to the formation of the All Manipur Students' Union.

III

The Constitution was known as Constitution of **All Manipur Students Union or Akhil Manipur Chhatra-Chhatri Sansthan.** The word **Manipur Students'** meant all the students studying in Manipur. The Constitution took into consideration of only the place of study. It took a non-Manipuri student reading in Manipur as a member of the Union. On the other hand, a student from Manipur reading outside the state Manipur was not entitled to be a member of the Union. The Constitution clearly promised to follow democratic and secular principles; colour, religion, place of birth of the student are not requirements to its membership.

There was a Preamble and eleven articles in the Constitution. There are two categories of membership __ permanent member and ordinary member. The representative of D.M. College, Imphal College, Manipur College and G. P. Women's College were recognised as the permanent members. All other will be treated as ordinary members[19]. The classification was made to make a distinction between the government and non-government educational institutions of that time. Some founder members of the Union while giving personal interview to the author expressed that the political power of the students rest with the permanent members. Decisions were taken in their favour. The post of the President was reserved for the permanent members.

A draft constitution (Amendment) was published in a souvenir (Hunger Marchers Day Observation) circulated by AMSU (Khelen) in 1980 considering emerging objectives conditions in the state. But it was only when Mongjam Abhiram Singh took charge as President of AMSU in 1983 a major amendment was done. It can be said that a new constitution, came into existence after the major amendment.

In the new constitution there is the Preamble, the body and two Annexures. There are 21 (twenty-one) articles. The Preamble reads *We the students of Manipur determined to unite to cooperate and to reaffirm faith in fundamental human rights and in co-existence and to advance progress in all the aspects of life, have resolved to unite our efforts to achieve these ends ; Accordingly our Representatives from several Academic institution from different parts of this state of Manipur assemble at Imphal do hereby constitute a Union to be known as* ***All Manipur Students' Union***.

Article III of the constitution declare that the All Manipur Students' Union shall have no alliance with any political party/organization and it shall stand to save the fundamental human rights, the aims and objectives as laid down in this constitution.

The increasing number of educational institutions in Manipur necessiated the amendment of the constitution. Personal interviews with ex-Executive Members of the union reveal that the new constitution tried to bring an integrated organization of the students community by removing the word permanent from the membership of the Union. Before the amendment, the post of the President was reserved for the permanent members of the Union. The amendment brought a new hope to the members of the Union. But the students favoured the student leaders who were in educational institutions of higher education. The elections, after the amendment showed that very clearly. Kh. Loken, the President of the Manipur University Student Council, became the President of the Union (1984-85). Since then the post of the President is seen as being practically reserved for the post-graduate student/university student. It continued till 1988. But Mr. Yenkokpam Priyokumar Singh of LMS Law College (President- LMS Law College Students' Union) became the President AMSU for the term 1988-89. Once more in the year 1989-90, Mr Lairenjam Gojendro Singh, President of Manipur University Students' Union became the President of the Union. This shows that the student of post graduate or higher studies have more potential to be President than the student reading in the schools and colleges.

The aim and objective of the Union, provided in Article IV of the constitution are as follows:

1. To achieve common ends through equality, fraternity and justice;
2. To protect and promote educational, social, cultural, physical. Moral, intellectual and scientific advancement on the general public and

students in particular through the spirit of unity, co-operation and selfless service;

3. To advance the practical significance of human welfare on the basis of democratic ideals;
4. To protect fundamental human rights.

Under Article VI of the Constitution there are four (4) classes of members. The student representative of the member institutions which participated and signed in the register of the general assembly meeting held on 12 September 1965 at Imphal shall be the **Founder Members** of the Union (Art.VI(1). Any *bonafide* representative of the educational institution right from High school or its equivalent upto the University level in Manipur which is affiliated to or recognised by AMSU shall become a member of the general assembly [Art.VI(2)]. University students were not members of the AMSU prior to the amendment of 3 May, 1984.

Article VI (3) says that any member of the General assembly if he/she is elected as a member of the Executive council shall automatically become a member of the Executive Council.

Any student of an affiliated/recognised educational institution shall be an ordinary member of the Union [Art.VI (4)].

Under Article VII the union shall have the following Administrative Organs namely:-

1. General assembly
2. Executive Council and
3. District Committees and such other committees

as may be formed by the Executive Council, from time to time.

Under article IX of the constitution provides that the administration of the Union shall be vested to an Executive Council consisting of a President, Vice-President, General Secretary, four Assistant Secretaries, Publicity and Information Secretary, Secretaries and one representative from each district committee.

Under Annexure-I(B)-(a) a candidate for any office of the Executive Council (i) shall be member of the General Assembly (ii) shall not be of unsound mind (iii) shall not be a member of any political parties or its students wing. Under annexure (B) - 9(b). A candidate for any office bearer of the President and the General Secretary of the Executive council shall in addition to qualifications mentioned in rule 9 (nine) above be student of Degree or equivalent or above.

Under article XI, the Executive Council shall meet as frequently as necessary with seven days notice and quorum of the meeting shall be one-third of the total members of the Executive Council. The term of the Executive Council as given under article XIV of the Constitution shall be one year in normal circumstances like occurrence of the National calamities, was, non-holding of school/college elections, its term shall be extend upto such time until a fresh election is held.

The power and functions of District Committee are given under article XIII of the Constitution as follows:-

1. There shall be a District Committee of the AMSU in each Administrative District of the state of Manipur consisting of a District President, a

District V.P., District Secretary, a Treasurer, Information Secretary and six other members its term shall be one year and shall be co-terminus with the term of the General Assembly.

2. The member of the District Committee shall be elected by the members of the General Assembly residing in the same district from among themselves. The word *residing* used in article XIII (2) signifies that the student should belong to the same district. It will also make easier to know the problem of the area if the student is a resident of the same district. The main function of the District Committee as given under article XIII (5) shall be to assist the Executive Council and the union for achieving its aims and objects. It also shall perform such other duties as may have the right to solve internal district problems in consultation with the Executive Committee by the new Constitution.

Under Article XIII (4) provides that the District Committee may meet as frequently as necessary and that its quorum shall be 1/5 of its total membership. The quorum given under this article is very small and any decision can be taken by 1/5 of its membership (without consulting the other members) Article XIII (6) of the Constitution it shall have the right to put forward proposals which are in time with the aims and objects of the union for consideration by the Executive Council.

The power and functions of the President are given under Article XV (1) of the Constitution (a) the President shall be the Head of the Union, (b) the President of the AMSU shall preside over all of the Executive Council, General Assembly and any other meetings of the AMSU.

Under Article XV (1) (d to h) of the Constitution, the President shall have the power to nominate observers in regard to the functioning of the District Committee/Sub-committee etc. In case of voting tie he/she have a casting vote. The president shall determine the items of business of the Executive Council in consultation with the Secretary General. The President may dissolve any committee or sub-committees etc. with the consent of the Executive Council.

The President and his Executive Council of 1985-86 took advantage of Article V (3) and Article VII (3) of the constitution by introducing Student Volunteer Committee to carry out their duties to solve the foreigner issue. They needed more units to mobilise and make the citizens or the students aware of the foreigners issue[20].

Under Article V (3) of the constitution, the union shall take up any programme, that is, deemed to be carried out at demand from time to time in conforming with the objectives of the union. Kongkham Brogen, the then President AMSU followed the fundamental principles of the union. Further article VII (3) of the constitution provides the District Committee and such time to time. The Union introduced units and branches of AMSU in every corner of Manipur. Personal interview with some members highlight that they were not in favour of the opening of new branches and units in every locality.

Under Article XXI provided any amendment of advancement of the constitution may be made by 2/3 of the general assembly. During 1984-85 when Kh. Loken was the president of the Union it adopted the following resolutions in a joint meeting of the AMSU and North District Students' Union.

1. To amend the Constitution of AMSU and

2. To include 3 (three) executive members of ATSUM (All Tribal Students' Union Manipur) in AMSU (July 6, 1985 at D.M. College of Science - DSI 1985 - 1747). But any amendment could not made during his tenure. It was a contradicting step to Article III of the constitution (Article III says - This constitution declares that the AMSU shall have no alliance with any political party/organization and it shall stand to save the fundamental human rights, the aims and objects as laid down in this constitution). And again it neglects Article VI (2) of the constitution. The tribal students too can become a member of the General assembly through their educational institutions. The membership of the union is open to all without any discrimination on the ground of caste, creed, colour, religion and place of birth. But he/she should be a student reading in any educational institution in Manipur.

Article XV (i) declared that the President shall be ordinarily be removed from his office without giving proper grounds. A 2/3 majority of the Executive Council or a 1/3 majority of the General Assembly may propose the removal.

The power and functions of the Vice-President is also provided under article XV (2) of the constitution. It says that the Vice-President will enjoy the power of the President in the absence of the President.

Election rules are given in annexure I (A) and (B) of the Constitution in detail, Annexure - I (A) (i) says there shall be an Election Committee consisting of (a) President of the Union' (b) General Secretary (c) Two members of the Executive Committee) d) Three other members to be nominated by President of the union.

Annexure I (A) (i) of the Constitution vested veto power to the President of the union. The executive council of the union is elected for every academic year. Because of the limited time given, the union faced many problems while implementing the annual policy and programmes of the union. That is why the Union mostly followed convention rather than the Constitution.

REFERENCES

1. *Encyclopedia Britanica,* Vol.16:975
2. Gabriel A Almond and G B Powell, Jr, *Comparative Politics,* Little Brown, London, 1978: 170
3. A Mitra, *Report on Inquiry of Police Firing at Imphal on 27-8-1965,* Manipur Legislative Assembly, Imphal, 1968: 7
4. *ibid.:* 12
5. *ibid.:* 14
6. *ibid.:* 50
7. A C Netrajit, *All Manipur Silver Jubilee 1965-1990 Souvenir,* AMSU, Imphal, 1990
8. Seymour M Lipset, "Students and Politics in Comparative Perspective" in P G Altbach, *op. cit.:* 34
9. Philip G Altbach, "Students and Politics" in *ibid.:* 52
10. Julian Nagel (ed), *Student Power,* Merlin Press, London, 1969
11. David Easton, "An Approach to the Analysis of Political System" in Stephen V Monsma and Jack R V D Slik, *American Politics,* Holt, New York, 1970: 9
12. Marion J Levy, Jr. *Modernization and The Structure of Societies,* Princeton University Press, New Jersey, 1966: 144
13. David Easton, *op. cit.:* 10
14. Neil Smelser, *Theory of Collective Behavior,* Glencoe, Ill., 1963: 491
15. David Easton, *op. cit.:* 10

16. Harold Lasswell, *Psychopathology and Politics,* University of Chicago Press, 1930: 78-80
17. Robert A Dahl, *Modern Political Analysis,* PHI, New Delhi, 1989: 116
18. see David Easton, *A System Analysis of Political Life,* John Wiley, New Delhi, 1965.
19. M C Arun, *Regional Integration,* Vol XVII-XIX, Imphal
20. Personal Interview with ex-members of the Union.

3

POLITICAL ACTIONS OF AMSU: FIRST TWO PHASES

The political action, like any other social action, is always goal-oriented; the goal may be deviant or conformist one for which the corresponding means, positive or negative, is being adopted by the actor(s). It is no general law that deviant goal has only negative means. So while looking at an interest group, it is necessary to examine the goal of the group and the means adopted. But one cannot ascertain the goal only through the observation of the group's manifest actions. Because of this AMSU is hereby observed to see the series of its demand and support as a unit of the political system of the state; while observing AMSU we consider the socio-cultural environment in which the Union is operating. AMSU has been exposing itself to various political changes in the post merger period and to various political movements such as socialist movement for full democratic legislature to Maoist movement for independent Manipur. As these movements are phenomena of different phases of contemporary history of Manipur, their impacts on political actions of AMSU are also qualitatively different. But the ideological sanction of AMSU i.e. neutrality to any political ideology and working on the basis or regionalism, does not mean that it would not do any political actions; such actions are motivated by the political inconsistency perceived by the masses. The need-disposition of largest section of the society is the basic guideline of such actions; but at final analysis in the practical sense, AMSU is supplied with political ideology of regionalism, **equality, human rights** by the elite circle of the society and AMSU acts accordingly. The ideology of ideological neutrality defines the position of AMSU in the system boundary of the polity in the state. AMSU can be kept itself free from the political parties.

In the present work, the history of AMSU is divided into four phases considering the role of AMSU in the political action system of larger state system and the need-disposition of the time. They are Phase I (1965-72) in which the demand of statehood dominated; Phase II (1972-77), a brief period that is marked by interest accumulation for 'demographic imbalance' issue; Phase III (1977-80) in which the slogan for secularism, micronationalism and demographic disequilibrium was the prime focus; Phase IV (1980-92) which was characterised by the interest accumulation for the language movement.

PHASEI: INDEPENDENCE OR STATEHOOD

The birth os AMSU in 1965 was not a gift of the students' community itself but a by-product of anti-congress movement and irresponsible congress government that worked jointly in an environment of economic chaos. Many latent political actions might have been operating in the State politics that resulted in the successive demonstrations against the Government Food policy in the middle week of August 1965.

The first two Executive Councils were actively demanding release of arrested students unconditionally and a judicial enquiry on the incident of 27 August '65. The Mitra

Commission was instituted. The Commission was conducted by Mr. A. Mitra, Additional Secretary, Planning Commission of India. The *examination of witnesses began on the morning of 27 October at the Imphal Dak Bungalow, continued every day and closed on the afternoon of 2 November when the list of witnesses was exhausted*[1]. The AMSU took a decision to boycott the Commission as it was not a judicial enquiry; but activists of AMSU including office bearers appeared before this Administrative inquiry. 27 students (19 males and 8 females) gave their eye witness accounts to the Commission. The students appeared included S. Lokendrajit, Kh. Ibetombi, Th. Gambhir. Kh. Joysakhi, L. Tombi, Sanajaoba Naoriya of the Executive Council of AMSU. They were nominated by the students on 12 September 1965. At the same time, protest rally and meetings were organised while the proceedings of the Commission was going on. Even on 12 October, AMSU mobilized a signature campaign among persons attaining 21 years of age, against the administrative inquiry and demanded a judicial inquiry. The Union sent a memorandum to Central Government. It is, however, notable that some of office bearers of AMSU appeared before Mr. Mitra who reached Imphal on 26 October 1965. In the Report, Mr. Mitra said, *Other witnesses who have testified to the incidents that occurred between the firing of the tear gas shells and the firing of rifles and how the crowd dispersed from the Chief Commissioner's compound are:*[2]

1. 20.10.65 Shri Angom Kula Singh of Wangkhei. Thambalkhong
2. 28.10.65 Smt. Sagolsem Ongbi Toyaima Devi of Wangkhei Konsam Leikai
3. 28.10.65 Smt. Sagolsem Ongbi Angoubi Devi of Wangkhei Konsam Leikai.

4. 2810.65 Shri Nongmaithem Manikchand Singh of Kongba Chandam Leikai.
5. 28.10.65 Shri A. Surendra Sarma of Brahmapur, Nahabam.
6. 28.10.65 Shri L. Tompok Singh of Chingamakha Kshreti Leikai.
7. 28.10.65 Shri Ningthoujam Budhi Singh of Thangmeiband
8. 29.10.65 Shri Soyam Syamsunder Singh, Kangabam Leikai.
9. 29.10.65 Shri Soyam Lokendrajit Singh, Kangabam Leikai.
10. 29.10.65 Shri Hidangmayum Mani Sharma, Bramhapur Nahabam Leikai.
11. 29.10.65 Shri Ksh Nabakumar Singh, Chingamathak, Nameirakpam Leikai.
12. 29.10.65 Shri Thokchom Manglem Singh, Wangkhei Ninghtem Pukhri Mapal.
13. 29.10.65 Shri Heisnam Joykumar Singh, Yumnam Leikai.
14. 29.10.65 Km. Kh. Ibetombi Devi, Ningthem pukhri Mapal.
15. 29.10.65 Km. Tongbram Bimola Devi, Kwakeithel Nganappi Thong.
16. 29.10.65 Km. Kh. Nomita Devi of Brahmapur Aribam Leikai.
17. 30.10.65 Shri P. Kula Sing, Student Manipur College.
18. 30.10.65 Shri Ksh. Tikendra Singh, Student D.M. College.

19. 30.10.65 Shri R.K. Pradip Singh, Student, Chingamakha High School.
20. 30.10.65 Km. Maibam Bimola Devi of Naharup Awang Leikai.
21. 1.11.65 Shri Koijam Jugeshwar Singh of Thoubal Wangma Taba, Thoubal.
22. 1.11.65 Shri S. Mohan Singh of Wangkhei Lourembam Leikai.
23. 1.11.65 Km. Ksh. Binasakhi Devi of Top Khongnangkhong.
24. 1.11.65 Shri W. Nabachandra Singh of Ahallup.
25. 1.11.65 Shri M. Birendra Sharma of Brahmapur.
26. 1.11.65 Shri Thingbaijam Lala Singh of Khurai Ningthoubung Leikai.
27. 2.11.65 Shri S.J. Naoriya, General Secretary, D.M.College.
28. 2.11.65 Shri Leisangthem Kumarjit Singh of Khurai Ningthoubung Leikai.
29. 2.11.65 Shri N. Ibohal Singh, Ex. Gen. Secy, Manipur College.
30. 2.11.65 Shri L. Tombi Singh, Ex. Gen. Secy, Manipur College.
31. 2.11.65 Shri Th. Gambhir sing Ex-Gen. Secy, Imphal College.
32. 2.11.65 Km. Joysakhi Devi, General secretary, Ghanapriya Women's College.

AMSU promptly responded to the call of the Nation as India entered into war against Pakistan in 1965. On 26 September the Union resolved to take part in the Civil Defence Training Camp, conducted at the Johnstone School[3].

The first conference comprising of Students from both plain and hills of Manipur was organised at D.M. College Complex on 28th July, 1967. The conference laid stress on three issues.

1. Mutual understanding and promotion of unity among the hills and plains students of Manipur.
2. The responsibility of students in the social welfare of the people.
3. Endeavour to meet the prevailing wants of students and other related matters[4].

One of the main activities of AMSU in 1969 were to check price hike at the time of Christmas. The businessmen charged higher prices illegally to large numbers of innocent people, coming from hill areas for Christmas shopping. Volunteers of AMSU engaged themselves in the market areas to check the price rise.

The main activities of Union in the 60's and early 70's were the demand for statehood and inclusion of Manipuri language in VIIIth Schedule of the Indian Constitution. Since 1967, AMSU began continuously demanding for a full-fledged statehood. At that time, the youth insurgency movement in Manipur had already started.

In spite of the resolution taken by the Union regarding the demand of statehood and inclusion of Manipuri in the VIIIth Schedule in 1966-67, it could not press the Indian Government with a full-interest strong determination as the organization was still in infancy. Being a new organization which lacked experience and a firm footing in any issue or problem, it was not an easy task to be taken up by the Union. While giving interview to the author, many executive members of the 60's and 70's expressed that AMSU did not take much initiative in the statehood demand. Rather they expressed its thankfulness to the Chief Minister for taking up the statehood issue with the Prime Minister and Home Minister, and also to the Samjukta Socialist Party and the Communist Party of India for their joint movement on the issue.

It was only in 1968-69, the interest accumulation reached a final stage and started its own movement to demand statehood. There were various democratic movements of political parties to the effect; AMSU also took part in the movement with its own colour as an important unit. For the first time in the history of AMSU, it boycotted the Republic Day Celebrations on 26 January 1969 pressing its demand for full-fledged statehood of Manipur and establishment of income generated industrial unit.

A similar case happened in Assam in the year 1968. The All Assam Student Union (Adhoc Committee) boycotted the Republic Day Celebration in 1963 as a protest against the centre's attitude on the question of state reorganisation[5]. AMSU used black flags to show its protest on the day. A leaflet reflecting idea of the Union said, *We the Manipuris participated in India's Republic Day Celebration with an open heart and joyful mind.... Instead of establishing industrial units, today Manipur has become a captive market of Indian goods by exploiting surplus rice (produced here). The outsiders are allowed to control the trade and commerce.... Unless safeguards, privilege and power is in our favour for the survival of Manipur, for the existence of many millions of Manipuri inhabiting in different parts of the globe is meaningless to participate in the Republic Day Celebrations*[6].

The demands of AMSU included among others the establishment of a Medical College, University of Manipur,

Agriculture College, Veterinary College, Engineering College etc. The Union placed their demands before the visiting University Grant Commission team at the Manipur Dramatic Union Hall Imphal on 3 March 1969 at a reception organised by the Union. The members of the Union expressed that the economic condition of the students did not allow them to go outside the state for further studies.

On 23 September 1969, Indira Gandhi, the Prime Minister of India visited Manipur. Youths and students organised a big rally as a part of their demand for a full fledged statehood. Socialist youths welcome the Prime Minister with a black flag which expressed their unhappiness towards the Government. It was the socialist element which influenced the youth in 1960's. AMSU too showed black flags and later it submitted a memorandum to demand statehood. It was signed by Achou Toijamba, President, AMSU. While addressing a public meeting at pologround, the then Prime Minister expressed *One of the gifts given to me on my way to this meeting from airport is statehood. But what I really want to know is, Do you think that you are fit for statehood by what you are doing now ? Do you think that the way you behave now is proper in front of your Prime Minister?* [7] While the Prime Minister was addressing the public, the youth and students began to set fire to public properties, pelting of stones. Amidst her speech, lathicharge was started on the youth and student demonstrators in front of the Johnstone School. In the police firing five persons, (1) R.K. Devendra Singh,(2) Kongbrailatpam Udhop Sharma, (3) Sanasam Jaichandra Singh (4) Laishram Nilkanta Singh and (5) Yumnam Samungou Singh were killed and also cause injury to many persons. The incident was a turning point in the political behaviour of the Union. On a later date, AMSU circulated a leaflet saying that *Will Manipur, once an independent state since the birth of the earth, die only because it loves India?*[8] After the incident of 23 September 1969, the Government of India imposed Presidents' Rule in Manipur.

Another focus of AMSU was the territorial integrity of Manipur. The question of territorial integrity of Manipur and statehood were raised at the same time. As a carrot and stick policy, India granted statehood to Nagaland in 1963 to appease the Naga underground. (Although statehood was conferred in January 1961 it was officially inaugurated in 1963). This made the Nagas of Manipur to raise a demand for Naga Integration. AMSU condemned the act of Mr. T.N. Angami, the then Chief Minister of Nagaland and the Naga elite of Manipur in 1968. The **Hindusthan Standard** dated 7 January 1969 reported that *The All Manipur Students' Union in the course of a memorandum lodged in protest with the Prime Minister against the demand made by the selected Naga leaders conference for merger of Naga inhabited areas of Manipur to Nagaland.*

On behalf of AMSU L. Saratchandra Sharma, President of the Union in a memorandum to the Prime Minister said that from time immemorial Manipur was a separate entity with its natural and geographical boundary remaining uninterrupted and its identity unchallenged. He also said that no Manipuri would tolerate this sort of interference in the internal affairs of Manipur and it would have serious consequences.

Saratchandra Sharma appealed to the Prime Minister to safeguard the territorial integrity of Manipur. However, he was not able to draw the attention of the general public to the issue. The problem was placed by Achou Toijamba on 26 May 1969 in a public meeting at Pologround, Imphal. In the meeting, all 30 MLAs of the time and public leaders were present and it discussed the problem of geographical integrity of the state.

An important dimension of political action of AMSU was the agitation safeguarding women's modesty in the state. It was the result of an indecent assault to a Meitei woman on 1 November 1970 by a Punjabi at around 5 p.m. in the streets of Imphal near a Cinema Hall in the presence of the members of her family and before the eyes of the big assembly of people. The day was **Ningol Chak-kouba,** a social festival of the Meiteis where Manipuri women were feted by their brothers at the family home, marking a once-in-a-year get-together.

There were riots in Imphal town the same night. The state government had to impose curfew in greater Imphal area to control the riot. Many student leaders and several youths were arrested after the incidents. AMSU took such arrests as a confrontation by the state. It staged several demonstrations demanding unconditional release of those arrested persons and a prompt judicial enquiry. Government resorted to arresting student demonstrators and abandoning them in far flung areas. On 11 November 1970, CRPF lathicharged demonstrators near the Singjamei bridge at Imphal. Again on 12th November, the police fired upon the student demonstrators. In order to pursue their demands, the students boycotted the celebration of the Children's Day on 14 November. AMSU appealed to the people to *remember Chacha Nehru at home.*

The agitation was, however, labelled by Samajbadi Yubajan Sabha as "a gift of self styled parties of Manipur and anti-social elements" to the state. The Sabha said that the office bearers of AMSU were influenced by the communal forces. It, however, demanded punishment for the culprit and unconditional release of the arrested persons. AMSU did not agree with the Sabha and denied their allegations.

AMSU came to a negotiation with Government of Manipur on 14th November. In a press note it said, *Whereas the Government have assured that on return of normalcy, prohibitory orders under section 144 of Cr.P.C. will be lifted, the educational institutions will be re-opened and the students arrested as a preventive measures will be released;*

The student community wants restoration of normalcy and it calls off its agitation. We further clarify that the student community never demanded unconditional release of all persons arrested, but only of innocent persons. The Government have promised early finalisation of investigation in the remaining cases and unconditional release of all persons against whom no case was made out.

In 1971 during the peak of the statehood movement, AMSU boycotted national festivals. In 1968-72 period, the main direction of AMSU political action was the grant of statehood to Manipur. A 1971 leaflet clearly showed the attitude of AMSU at that time. It said, *It is our stand that the Manipur students will not participate in any national festival until Manipur is granted statehood and Manipuri language is included in the Schedule VIII of the Constitution of India.*

PHASE II: INTEREST ACCUMULATION FOR DEMOGRAPHIC ISSUE

Five persons died on 23 September 1969 during the Statehood movement. There were rallies, hunger strikes, public meetings and different forms of **Bandh** organised by AMSU and the Statehood Demand Co-ordinating Body (comprising

Congress CPI, SSP, PSP, CPM and MPP; later MNO and Congress-O joined). Even there was a civil disobedience programme from 17 August to 28 August 1970. On 6 September 1970, the Union Minister for Home Affairs and the Prime Minister announced in the Parliament that Manipur and Tripura would be granted statehood. Accordingly, the **North Eastern Area (Re-organisation) Act 1971** was passed in December 1971 and enforced on 21 January 1972 (vide GSR 1B(E) dated 6-1-72, Gazette of India Extraordinary Sec 3(1) p.57).

As the statehood issue came to an end, AMSU was, for a while, politically inactive. But, it can be noted that AMSU did exert pressure on 26 February 1972 for announcing general amnesty to the **political prisoners** who were arrested in connection of underground activities and lodged in different jails in and outside the state. AMSU said, *Is it not time to look after the youths of Manipur who are suffering in different jails ? Like in other countries, they should be granted general amnesty on the attainment of statehood.* Simultaneously all the political parties were also demanding general amnesty to all political offenders. As a consequence, all cases registered against the Manipuri youths involved in political offences were withdrawn and all political offenders in jail custody were released as a result of the general amnesty. Though the pressure of AMSU was not the sole factor, general amnesty was granted to all the undertrial insurgents who were arrested or wanted by the Government of Manipur on 5 June 1972. In the aftermath, AMSU took initiative in demanding lower income scholarship for the students, price control and beautification of Imphal (restoration of Kangla Moat) etc. .

In this phase, AMSU started to accumulate a serious interest in the demographic aspects of politics. In a memorandum submitted to the then Advisor to the Governor of Manipur on 25 July 1973, the AMSU President Kh. Doren Meitei drew attention of the authorities on the problem. He wrote - *the population of Manipur is increasing by leaps and bounds. The own production of the state and the Government distribution cannot meet the requirements of the people. Due to food scarcity, natural calamities and shortage of everything, struggle for existence has become more crucial. Common life is in danger. People in all walks of life are not getting two square meals a day, without exaggeration.*

In such a situation, the ceaseless inflow of refugees and outsiders in Manipur is creating problems, social disorder and exploitation.... When the state was more than self-sufficient there was no voice for restriction to outsiders and they were all well afforded.

Therefore, in order to protect the economically backward people, to preserve their identity and to free them from exploitation, refugees and outsiders should not be allowed to enter the state without proper justification.

The same point was once again emphasized by another resolution of the Executive Council of AMSU, which was submitted to the Advisor, Government of Manipur on 27 August 1973. Copies were sent to the Prime Minister and the Home Minister of India. Out of the 6 resolutions passed, the Resolution 4 read: *Refugee influx should be checked immediately in the interest of the people of Manipur. Any disregard to this view will follow serious consequences of political, economic and social. Any outsider in Manipur can never be allowed to settle permanently just to save the interest of the minority people of Manipur.*

However, mobilization on the 'Demographic' Issue was delayed because of two incidents. First, the Police firing on the agitating students of Moirang Multipurpose Higher Secondary School on 27 September in pursuit of their 16 point Charter of demands submitted to the Director of Education, Government of Manipur, for the betterment of their school. In the firing, a student namely Haobijam Ibohal of Ningthoukhong died. Second, the communal tensions over a **Mayang** (outsider from mainland India) shopkeeper's act of molestation of a Manipuri woman on 13 September, 1973.

An application submitted by Kh. Ibetombi, General Secretary of MACHA LEIMA (a womens' organisation) and L. Chitra, General Secretary of G.P. Women's College Students Union to the then Superintendent of Police (Central) alleged that, *on September 13, 1973 at 3 p.m. one Memtombi was molested by a Marawari shopkeeper at Paona Bazar, Imphal.* Copies were sent to AMSU, Pan Manipur Youth League, Shri Chhibber, Advisor to the Government of Manipur, Associated Chamber of Commerce Manipur, All Manipur Women's Association and Kangleipak Women's Association.

AMSU in an emergency meeting of the Executive Council held on 16 September unilaterally formed a Peace Committee under four conditions (1) withdrawal of curfew and 144 CrPC in Imphal area, (2) release of the arrested youths and students in connection with the 13 September incident, (3) opening of all the educational institutions and (4) all responsiblity for any ontoward incident to the culprit who molested the woman. Then, it submitted a 7 point charter of demands on 24 September with a 30 September dateline. On 8 October, AMSU launched a relay hunger strike to press their demands.

1. Withdrawal of 144 CrPC from the Imphal Municipality area;
2. To release the youths and students arrested in connection with the last 13th September incident;
3. Drastic action against the persons who molested a woman and that he should be held responsible for the unfortunate incident of 13th September;
4. Constitute of judicial enquiry on the 13 September incident;
5. Government should give teaching facilities to the aided school students who have been affected by the cease work strike of the All Manipur Secondary Teachers' Association and immediate redressal of teachers demands;
6. Withdrawal of CRPF personal from the state;
7. Immediate stop to mass raids and arrests in connection with the 13 September incident.

The riot was reported in various sections of the press. A report in IHOU daily said - *at Thangal Bazar, from shopkeepers' side more than 13 rounds of bullets were fired... Some outsiders burnt down their own shops, it is reported.* Another Manipuri daily PAOJEL said, - *During the curfew hours in nightfall, at Thangal Bazar... a group of persons shouted' Manipur Police Murdabad, CRPF Zindabad... all the suspected persons who were arrested were Manipuris, no outsiders was arrested on suspicion.* The reports reflect a vivid account of the incident infused with local sentiment.

AMSU made its stance clear on the Enquiry instituted to look into the 13 September incident, in a memorandum submitted to the Union Home Minister and Parliamentary Consultative Committee on their visit to Manipur on 23 November. It said, -

> Inspite of repeated demands from the public, the Government of Manipur has recently appointed Shri L.B. Thanga, Revenue Commissioner as Enquiry Officer to institute an enquiry into the incident confining to a 5-point terms of reference only and the period of enquiry beginning with the molestation of woman to the time at about 4.30 p.m. on the day of the incident... It does not enquire into the incident of burning of shops and the properties of market women worth about 20 lakhs and killing of innocent persons at Paona Bazar and Thangal Bazar, after the imposition of curfew and deployment of Army in the Imphal Municipality area...

In this connection, the action of the authorities concerned is unwarranted and unjust. Many innocent youths were arrested and harassed in the jail without a shrd of evidence of their involvement .. On the other hand, not a single non-Manipuri who fired gun shots wounding two innocent Manipuris and also those who violated curfew, except the accused who molested the Manipuri woman, was arrested. During Presidents' Rule, the action of the authority concerned is very communal and the Manipuris have been treated as foreigners in their own land.

Meanwhile, the suspension of subordinate Police officers who performed duty to the best of their ability with a limited hand to save the accused person and also to control the whole situation is not justified, as the Enquiry officer has not yet submitted the findings of his enquiry which will determine the final decision of the whole situation. While doing so, the responsible officials of the Police Department were excluded by the enquiry whether by high level conspiracy or favouritism. We condemn all such acts of ill-treatment by the Government.

It is obvious that, the AMSU stand reflects the general

attitude of the Manipuris towards the **Mayangs** (the outsiders). Generally, a Manipuri thinks that the **Mayangs** are the *de-facto* controllers of Manipur's economy who in turn are protected by the state forces. Out of the students' fear of inferior position of Manipuris in their own state and out of their micro-nationalist feeling, widespread violence became manifest in the wake of molestation of a Manipuri woman by a Marawari man. But, it was not a communal act, rather an irresponsible **Mayang** shopkeeper who tried to play with fire.

Athough there were agitations on the issue of scholarships for the lower income group, conversion of LMS Law College as a Government College, increase in MBBS seats in the Regional Medical College of Imphal, no serious political action could be seen in this period. During the Emergency (1975-77), like political parties and other social groups in the state AMSU could not do anything. They even did not conduct its own election and remained inactive for about two years.

REFERENCES

1. A Mitra, *Report on Inquiry of Police Firing at Imphal on 27-8-1965,* Manipur Legislative Assembly, Imphal, 1968: 7
2. ibid.,: 7
3. see *Hunger Marchers' Day Sovenier,* 27 August, 1967, All Manipur Students' Union, Imphal
4. ibid
5. Meeta Deka, *NEIHA Proceeding of 14th Sesssion*, Shillong, 1993
6. Free translation of the leaflet in Manipur
7. NK Sanajaoba (ed). *Lamyanba,* Manipuri monthly, Pan Manipuri Youth League, Imphal, November, 1969
8. *Hueiyen Lanpao,* a Manipuri daily, Statehood Day Special Issue, 21 January 1996

4

AMSU AND SECULARIZATION OF EDUCATION

During the period of national emergency (1975-1977), AMSU could not take up any programme including its Executive Council elections. The Executive Council led by Ayekpam Dijen Meitei as President had therefore to hold the office for about two years. The Elections for the next Executive Council was held on 4 December 1977. With the advent of the new Executive Council for the year 1977-78, AMSU entered its third phase. In this phase there were three Executive Councils. The first two Executive Councils were led by Kh. Kuleshwar and H. Bijoy. The third Executive Council split with one faction led by Maisnam Khelen and the other by L. Dilip as Presidents.

The major activities of the AMSU, during 1978-79, was the abolition of religious functions from the educational institutions. Here it may not be out of place to mention that the Manipuris were converted into Vaisnavite Hinduism in the first half of the eighteenth century during the reign of Maharaja Garibaniwaj (1709-1748). However, "Meetei" revivalists became very strong and wanted to denounce the conversion to Hinduism. Many ex-members of the Union were also sympathetic to the revivalist movement. At the same time, the Sanamahi Temple Board contributed much in reviving the Meitei religion and culture. They published many pamphlets and booklets regarding the Meitei Religion, its culture and traditions. The first sign of success of religious revivalism in Manipur could be seen in the restoration of Lainingthou Sanamahi in the year 1978 at Haying Khongbal[1]. Some felt, it was a challenge to Hinduism. However, it was also a fact that the children of the Vaisnavite parents later became members of the Meitei Marup. Many others who were once devotees of Vaisnavism were converted to Meitei Marup (Sanamahi). A large number of factors contributed to the revivalist movement. Among the causes, a group was of the opinion that the Meiteis were converted into Hinduism against the will of the people. It was substantiated by new writings revealing the past. In another sense, denunciation of Hinduism was considered to be an important factor for building up national identity. Events cited herein are some of the evidences to substantiate it. Moreover, students were largely influenced by the revivalist movement and many students also become new converts.

Saraswati Puja was the most popular celebration of the students' community in Manipur during the 1950's and 1960's. In most of the cases, the celebrations continued for about three or four days. On the first day, the image of the goddess Saraswati was brought from the house of the idol maker to the educational institution with the participation of almost all the students of the school and in most of the cases with a band party. Then the **Puja** was started. Some refreshments were also given. After that, a series of activities like literary competitions, cultural items, games and sports were organised. Meritorious students were awarded during the celebration. The celebrations were held with contribution from the students both in the schools and colleges. The celebration was no doubt associated with the Hindu Goddess of Learning Saraswati, and the influence most probably came from Bengal.

It was during the AMSU President Khangembam Cha Kuleswar that the issue was brought into focus. AMSU charged that, such religious functions are organised in the educational institutions with contribution made compulsory by the state from the students. Manipur, being a part of secular India, should not encourage such religious functions in the educational institutions. The Union also defied the collection of contribution with regard to such religious functions. Some former members of the union argued that, it was not the Government who was collecting the money from the students but the parents organisations who had taken the initiative of organising the **Pujah**. However, many were of the opinion that "when Manipur became a full-fledged state under India, the people became aware of their rights for preservation of tradition and culture. They published many pamphlets, booklets and leaflets regarding Meitei religion, culture and tradition.

A meeting of AMSU held on 15 February 1978 at Manipur College resolved among other things (1) to check frequent religious holidays in schools and (2) to resist collection of fees with regard to religious functions. On 3 March 1978, a memorandum was submitted to the Chief Minister. The demands included (1) Correction of the wrong History of Manipur and the teaching of corrected history of Manipur upto Class X; (2) Establishment of a full fledged University in Manipur; (3) Instruction of a Meitei script and inclusion of Manipuri Language in the VIII Schedule of the Indian constitution; (4) Abolition of religious functions from educational institutions (abolition of subscription for **Pujah** etc. and holidays on religious functions should be stopped except Sunday); (5) No difference should be made between Government Aided and Government colleges at the time of reimbursement of tuition fees; (6) Let the morning shift classes be allowed to continue; and (7) (a) To reduce bus fares and (b) To reduce prices of essential commodities.

Accordingly, the Executive Council was empowered by the General Body Meeting held on 9 March 1978 to take up actions for realisation of the demands. After submitting its memorandum, AMSU gave the Government 2 months time to consider its demands with an ultimatum dated 3 August. Side by side, it started to mobilise the general population to this effect.

The foundation of the activities of AMSU in this phase lies in the resolution of its Executive Council on 18 July 1978 and the memorandum of 25 July 1978 (Earlier at a General Body meeting held on 9 March, 1978 the executive council was empowered to take up action). The resolutions of the meeting was a serious attempt to alter the then existing social ideology. The Government was pressurized to take a decision for altering the ideological culture of the state. It resolved that "any religious function, money collection, holidays and any secretary in the name of religion must be abolished from the educational institutions. Educational institutions should not be bound by any monastic rules"[2].

While these steps were being take up, the boycott of Saraswati **Puja** in the educational institutions had already been started with a resolution of Executive Council adopted on 15 February 1978. The main arguement of the boycott was that, a secular country like India should not allow religious festivals to be organised in the educational institutions. In some of the leaflets, it was reflected that Hinduism was the main cause that led to the **"wrong history of Manipur"**. A leaflet read as: "*without teaching the high ideals of Hindu philosophy, the people was divided* *with the polluted concept which has created tension between the different social groups with the change of our seven clans to nine gotras with the false claim of Aryan origin of the Meiteis ... what we gain by abolishing Saraswati* **Pujah** *is the liberation of many religious sects from the Hindu Yoke".*

AMSU banned Saraswati Pujah in the educational institutions and even local celebrations. The State Police Department tried its utmost to suppress the movement. Police officials even started collecting signatures of the parents declaring that they would prevent their wards from participating in any strike or agitation.

The agitation was intensified in the month of August 1978 after the lapse of the August 3 ultimatum. AMSU used its usual technique of mass demonstrations here and there in Greater Imphal. On 18 August, a group of students numbering about 450 gathered at the gate of the Chief Minister's bungalow shouting slogans in support of their demands. The same was repeated on 23 August and they even picketed the Chief Minister's office. When four representatives of AMSU met the Chief Minister Yangmaso Shaiza, no solution could be reached. After the talks failed, violent actions followed. On 24 August, a Manipur State Transport bus (MNS 9625), a car belonging to the Education Department (MNS 8165), and a truck of PWD (MNS 1391) were set on fire in different places of Imphal. The same day, it was reported that 9 youths were rounded up by police. Next day a jeep of the Manipur Apex Co-operative Marketing Society (MNS 8534) was set on fire by a group of 10 students but no damage was done. On 28 August, AMSU staged another procession of students numbering about 500 students from different parts of Greater Imphal. Unable to control the demonstration, the police fired upon the student demonstrators, although no one was seriously injured. Police arrested 33 students in the melee.

On 29 August, AMSU condemned the act of firing as irresponsible and sign of inefficiency of the police. A pressnote said, *"Why should the students be fired upon when they were demanding that no wrong history should not be taught, no* **Pujah** *should be compulsory in educational institutions, teach us our own script, establish a full-fledged university, bringing down the price of essential commodities ?"* It further added *"Where is our freedom if we are fired upon for saying we like lessons irom our own history, secularism and our own script ?"*

In a letter despatched by AMSU to the then Prime Minister, Government of India (Ref.No. 17/AMSU/8 dated 29 August, '78) it accused Y. Shaiza, the then Chief Minister of Manipur saying that *"instead of looking into the matter and solving the problems the state government is trying to suppress student unrest by firing upon the students at 2.20 p.m. on the 29th August, 1978"*.

The circumstances in which the police resorted to firing on 29 August was dubbed as a "historical blunder" by the student community. The police strongly asserted that, there was no other alternative as the number of students who joined the demonstration had swelled. According to their account, about one thousand students from different schools and colleges was staging a procession in front of the New Secretariat building. They were shouting slogans and demanding the release of arrested students. Another group of about 500 students were also approaching the spot from the southern direction. The Manipur Rifles personnel tried to stop them on the way. There was confusion among the security personnel. When some students tried to set on fire the fuel tank of a jeep, police opened fire at 2.30 p.m. Angry students pelted stones that caused damage to a jeep belonging to the Department of National Survey. That day, eleven students were arrested on the spot. Nobody was reportedly injured, however, in the firing. To control the situation, the State Government imposed 144 CrPC in Imphal Municipality area and closed all the educational institutions from 30 August to 8 September 1978.

A government press note was released by the Secretary, Education Department on 31 August stating Government's unilateral decision on 7 points. It included:

(1) correction of the wrong history of Manipur and corrected history would be introduced upto Class X (*"the Government had appointed a Committee of 3 Scholars to examine the lessons in history of Manipur now being taught in different High and Higher schools of Manipur. The Committee would submit its report within 3 months time"*).

(2) Instruction of Meitei script and inclusion of Manipuri language in the VIII Schedule to the Constitution (*"the Government will make efforts to adopt the universally accepted version of the Old Manipuri script. The appointment of the Research Scholars will be made latest by 31st October, 1978. Regarding the inclusion of Manipuri language in the VIII Schedule of the Constitution the matter was raised with the Central Government. The Parliament is the only competent authority to decide this matter"*).

(3) Abolition of religious functions from educational institutions (*"In accordance with the provisions of the Constitution of India the freedom of worship has been assured as one of the Fundamental Rights. Demands for not granting holidays for religious functions and worship would be unconstitutional. In so far the collection of subscription is*

concerned the Government have issued no orders for collection of any type of subscription for any religious functions. The Government had also not asked to hold any religious function").

On the abolition of religious functions in the educational institutions, the September agreement explicitly expressed that *"It was agreed that the appointment of Moral and Religious Secretaries in various schools and colleges should be discontinued forthwith. Any religious function, money collection in the name of religion must be barred in educational institutions"*.

Regarding the 'correct' history of Manipur, by an order of the Governor of Manipur (No.1/PA/SSE-78 dated August '78), three scholars, namely S. Kunjabihari Singh, Principal, Manipur College; Gangumei Kabui, JNU Centre, Imphal and A. Lokendra Singh, Senior Lecturer, D.M. College of Arts and Commerce, Imphal were appointed to examine the contents of History books. They were directed to submit the report within three months.

On 7 September, the representatives of AMSU and the Government of Manipur came to an agreement. The signatories were Kh. Kuleshwar, President AMSU; I. M angi, General Secretary AMSU; N. Achouba, Publicity Secretary AMSU; Ratankumar Thouna, Advisor, AMSU; and M D Tyagi, Secretary (Education), Government of Manipur. The agreement consisted of 4 points:-

1. Instruction of Meitei script and inclusion of Manipuri language in the VIII Schedule of the Constitution.
2. Abolition of religious functions in educational institutions.

3. Adoption of one village by each college for understanding development.
4. Establishment of an Engineering College in Manipur.

After the agreement, the celebration of Saraswati **Pujah** in educational institutions was abolished. Although some institutions continued to celebrate the **Pujah** for about 2/3 years more, religious functions in educational institutions was altogether banned. That was a great achievement for the Union.

Though the main agitation came to an end, the Executive Council of 1977-78 took up certain interests which were actively articulated in some sections of the population. In a meeting held on 3 October 1978, AMSU once again took up the geographical integrity issue. Next day, the President of AMSU sent a letter to the Prime Minister of India, a portion of which read as:

It is also my duty to inform you that the recent statements of Rano Shaiza, MP from Nagaland and T Sailo, Chief Minister of Mizoram demanding the integration of the Naga and Mizo inhabited areas into Nagaland and Miroram have greatly excited the minds of the people of Manipur.

The people of Manipur in general and the student community in particular feel that, under the circumstances, a categorical assurance from the Prime Minister of India within October 15, 1978 to the effect that the statements in question only reflect the personal opinions of Rano Shaiza and T Sailo and that Government of India stands committed to preserve the territorial integrity of Manipur is in order.

If such an assurance is not forthcoming within October 18, 1978 the All Manipur Students' Union would be compelled to take the stand for the separation of Manipur from the Indian Union. I hope the Hon'ble Prime Minister will not drive us to this extreme step.

Two more memoranda were submitted to the Prime Minister on 4 October and 5 November in Imphal. The demands were:

1. Safeguarding the Territorial integrity of Manipur;
2. Withdrawal of the Armed Forces (Assam and Manipur) Special Powers Act, 1958;
3. Stop Nepali influx in the tribal areas;
4. Establishment of Agriculture College and Manipur University.

Though copies were sent to the different authorities, AMSU did not take the adopted resolutions to the streets. But as a positive outcome, AMSU suceeded in bringing to focus the importance of regional history of Manipurin various political and academic circles.

At the end of its tenure, AMSU (1977-78) organized a conference on **The Study of Regional History of Manipur** on 16-19 February, 1979 at the premises of the Raja Dumbra Singh High School, Imphal. The conference was attended by students, teachers, educationists and scholars. Two main resolutions were adopted by the Conference:

Conscious of the composite contribution of many ethnic groups and the regional history of Manipur;

Believing in the inter-relationship of the history and culture of different peoples; and

Desirous of preventing the harmful effect of teaching a distorted regional history of Manipur on the students;

The Conference resolved that

1. The Government of Manipur and the other authorities concerned be urged to introduce from the academic session beginning 1980 a systematic and objective study and teaching of the regional history of Manipur in all classes in all educational institutions of the state;
2. Resolved that the following topics be invariably included in the syllabi of all classes as part of the social studies and/or history subjects with appropriate modifications to suit the varying standards of different classes:
    a. Advent of Poireiton in Manipur valley;
    b. Consolidation and evolution of Meitei or Meetei identity from different clans (*Yeks and Salais*);
    c. Advent of Hindu religion in Manipur during Pamheiba's reign and the consequent schism in Meitei/Meetei society;
    d. **Chahi Taret Khuntakpa** (1819-1826) as a watershed in the regional history of Manipur ;
    e. The British political agency and the growth of colonial influence and British conquest of Manipur in 1891;
    f. Advent of Christian influence in Manipur's hill area ;
    g. The Kuki Rebellion (1917-19) ;
    h. 'Nupee Lan' (1939) (Women's agitation) and the colonial exploitation of Manipur under British Raj;

i. Manipur's relations with Ahoms, Angami, Cachharis, Lushais, Tripuris, Akamhwas and Burmese.

LIST OF VIOLENT ACTIONS

Date	*Place*	*Nature*	*arrest, if any.*
24 August	Wangkhei	Set fire Bus MNS 9625	4
24 August	Chingamathak	Set fire Car MNS 8165	1
24 August	Haobam Marak MNS 1391	Set fire truck	1
25 August	Elangbam Leikai	Set fire jeep MNS 8534	
30 August	Chingamathak	Set fire vehicle of P/T department.	

During the year 1978-79, AMSU did not bring up any new issue or follow-up action on the policies of the last Executive Council. AMSU reacted strongly to the police firing on the students of Moirang Multipurpose Higher Secondary School on 28 May 1979. In the firing, one student named Uritkhinbam Khelchandra (16) died on the spot and three others were injured. Another student named Kumam Saratchandra (14) succumbed to injuries.

In a press statement issued on 31 May 1979, Ngangbam Nongyai, the General Secretary of AMSU condemned the police action at Moirang saying that the killing of two students at Moirang on 28 May 1979 in police firing was an open challenge to the students community. The Union demanded punishment of the police personnel responsible for the killing and immediate fulfilment of the demands of the students. Other demands were:

(i) unconditional release of five students arrested on 27 May;

(ii) compensation to the families of the deceased & injured students;

(iii) fulfilment of rightful demands of the students;

(iv) judicial enquiry into the police firing;

(v) proper action against N. Ibohal Singh, O.C. Moirang P.S.;

(vi) withdrawal of section 144 CrPC from Moirang area; and

(vii) re-opening of schools and colleges.

Ngangbam Nongyai, the General Secretary along with three other members went to Moirang on 1 June to observe the situation. They found that members of Communist Party of India, National Students Union of India, All India Youth Federation and All India Students Federation were responsible for the situation leading to the police firing. They reiterated their demands for fulfilment within 3/4 months. The union also decided to negotiate with the Chief Minister. However, there was no follow-up action.

On 11 June 1979, a meeting of the Executive Council was held with Kh. Babu in the chair at the premises of the Johnstone Higher Secondary School which resolved to demand:

(a) Introduction of Meitei script from the next academic session;

(b) Introduction of new history of Manipur as a subject from next academic session in all educational institutions as decided in the last AMSU regional conference held at R.D.S. High School on 16-19 February, 1978;

(c) Minimisation of holidays in educational institutions;

(d) Inclusion of Manipuri in the VIII Schedule of the Constitution;

(e) Establishment of a full-fledged University in Manipur;

(f) Fixation of price of essential commodities;

(g) To allot land for the construction of an office of the Union and

(h) Introduction of different cultural programmes in AIR, Imphal.

Despite the demands put forward by the Union before the Government, the executive committee of the Union (1979-80) led by W. Bijoychandra (President, AMSU) did not take up any follow up action to press their demands. There were memoranda in this regard but no overt political action could be seen. But, during this period some interest could be accumulated outside the routine AMSU activities.

REFERENCES

1. W Ibemu Devi, *Meitei Revivalism in Manipur,* unpublished thesis, Manipur University, 1991
2. Personal interview, Kh Kuleshwar

5

FOREIGNERS ISSUE

I

At the end of tenure of the Executive Council of 1978-79, there was a confusion over the elections of the next Council. Two elections were conducted on different dates by different authorities of AMSU, resulting in two factions. Under the authority of President W Bijoychandra and Vice President Kh. Babu of 1978-79 term, an election was held on 26 February, 1980. In the said election, the following office bearers were elected:

1.	Meisnam Khelen	President
2.	H Biramani	Vice-President
3.	Kh Babu Meitei	General Secretary
4.	Ksh Monoranjan	Finance Secretary

The validity of the election was challenged by Ng Nongyai, General Secretary of 1978-79. So, there were claims and counter-claims of each being the real AMSU. Like in the case of political parties, no one could say which one was the real AMSU.

Many student groups tried in vain to unite the warring factions. A leaflet circulated by "All Students of Manipur" on 2 April, 1980 appealed "*The AMSU split has confused the students. Now, we, the students like to know which one is the real AMSU ... As All Manipur Students' Union is AMSU, the name should not be used to denote either of the factions."* A. Noutuneshwari, General Secretary of G P Women's Colege Students' Union, and Th Indrajit Singh, Finance Secretary of N G College Students' Union personally initiated a meeting on 8 April. The meeting was attended by the representatives of 46 schools and colleges. It resolved to organise a common forum of the representatives of both factions. So, another meeting was held on 12 April at the Central Hall of D M College of Science which was attended by representatives of both the factions, officials of the All Manipur Students' Co-ordinating Committee (AMSCOC, another student forum), different school and college students' unions, and many ex-office bearers of AMSU. In spite of the efforts, both factions refuse to re-unite and started to move in their own ways.

Although there were differences between the two factions, they had a common demand. Both factions decided to protect the state from the "foreigners" and both exerted various political pressures for their demand.

II

An issue which was taken up by AMSU vigorously was the "Foreigners issue". Before we start discussing this particular issue it is better to have a clear understanding of how the issue was built up, politicised and shaped into a movement. For the movement survived for a long time.

It is a fact that India's neighbours Bangladesh and Nepal are poorer than India, Therefore, it is but natural for people from these countries to keep on moving from place to place in search of fortune and better opportunities. The same is true with the Bangladeshis and Nepalese. Therefore, there has been reports that there is influx of foreigners from these areas in particular to the northeast India. In this connection, at least two influential organizations the All Manipur Students' Union (AMSU) and the All Assam Students' Union (AASU) were vocal.

AMSU's stand on the influx was based on certain data available to them. It contended that the decadal rate of population growth in 1971 census was found in Manipur much higher than the national average. In 1971, the national figure of decadal growth was 19 per thousand while it was 37.53 in Manipur. The figure was comparatively higher even then some of the states in the northeast India. For example, Assam had 34, Meghalaya 31.5. Again the real growth in population in Manipur was 2,93,170 in 1901-1951; but in the next 10 years period, the figure jumped up dramatically. In 1951 it was 5,77,000 and in 1961, it come up more than 8 lakhs.

The number of foreigners was 1,42,033 in 1961-71 out of which 67,688 were females and 74,345 males. The district wise break up of foreigners in 1971 census was as follows:-

1.	North District	-	16,048
2.	East District	-	5,400
3.	West District	-	2,980
4.	Tengnoupal District	-	5,523
5.	South District	-	18,408
6.	Central District	-	23,674

The age group of the immigrants in 1961-71 is a vital clue to the study of demography of the state. The age wise distribution is hereby given below:

Age group	*Male immigrant*	*Female immigrant*
10 - 19	33,424	37,398
20 - 29	11,682	10,107
30 - 39	4,820	1,105
40 - 49	5,309	4,280
50 - 59	6,374	5,038
60 - 69	6,310	4,925
70 and above	6,426	7,045
Total	**74,345**	**67,688**

The figure shows that the largest number of foreigners are in the group of 10-29. The number of immigrants decreases when the age increases. On the other hand the AMSU projected population of Manipur for 1986 would be high 2 (2.20 lakh), high 1 (28 lakhs), medium 2 (2.09 lakhs), low 2 (2.09 lakhs), low 2 (1.93 lakhs), low 1 (1.88 lakhs), i.e. the total number would be 12.41 lakhs. This would constitute about 15.19 percent of the total population. Moreover, the population density in the valley region (2240 sq.km.) was 325 against the national figure of 182. The high rate of population, thus caused 'ecological imbalance, economic deterioration, and socio-cultural chaos in the state'.

As population increases, it warned the number of agriculturists would be about 3,48,000 in 1986 (projected) and would demand 1,91,000 hectares of cultivable fields. This would also create more pressure on cultivable land and homestead land.

Considering the above basic statistics, both the factions of AMSU, like other political parties, were concerned about the future of the Manipuris. Both the factions of AMSU did not differ much in the way how they looked at the issue. Both were alarmed with the disproportionate increase of Nepalis, Bengali Muslims from Bangladesh and an uncertain future dominated by these foreigners. A Meitei proverb *'Lam mapu yongna tanba'* [Monkeys driving out the land owner] was the main motivational factor.

Both the factions published many leaflets charged with emotion and sentiment for mass awareness of the 'future shock'. Not only these sentimentally dominated leaflets, some booklets were also published to convince the people rationally. In the later form, they employed census data and projected them to support and justify their arguments of 'the problem'.

A leaflet circulated by N. Budhachandra, Editor AMSU (Khelen) appealed, *"Those persons who do not like the death of the Manipuris at the hands of increasing foreigners should agree to the 'AMSU's stand and join the fight against these foreigners."*

A booklet issued by the Joint Publicity Section of AMSU(Dilip) and AMSCOC also states, *"Problem of influx of immigrants into the north eastern region is a national problem. Laudable efforts to safeguard our constitution through deletion of the foreigners from the electoral rolls has been misrepresented as communal or chaotic agitation. As a result the movement to preserve the identity and ethos of Manipuris has been misrepresented. This movement is the struggle of Manipuris to save their hearth and home from a silent civilian invasion by herds of illegal immigrants from Bangladesh, Nepal and Burma. The whole population of India must be against neo-colonial policy of foreigners state.*

H. Biramani, Vice-President AMSU (Khelen) said, *"the problem has now created apprehension and panic in the minds of the original inhabitants. They are haunted by the constant fear of being outnumbered and uprooted from their homeland."* The matter was brought to the notice of the Government of Manipur. The Government of India was also apprised, time and again, by the Kuki National Assembly, Manipur but they paid no heed. The Kuki National Assembly, Manipur entered into an agreement with the United Legislative Party government (a coalition government headed by Md. Alimuddin) on 1 August 1972 which said, *"the Nepalis should be struck off from the voters list. But, only lip service was paid and this was not carried out in practice.... Being a kind of secret invasion, this has to be tackled now as a national problem. Any patriotic Indian should support this movement for the national cause instead of branding it as an anti national one... The Indo-Nepal treaty of Peace and Friendship of 1950 under Articles 6 and 7 allowed Commercial Rights to the Nepalese and not political rights".*

An Executive Meeting of AMSU (Khelen) with Kh Kuleshwar, Chairman of the Advisory Board of this Union was held on 10 March, 1980 and decided to submit a memorandum to the Chief Minister of Manipur urging him to fulfil the following demands within fifteen days. The memorendum was submitted to the Chief Minister of Manipur and the Prime Minister of India on 10 March. The charter of demands include:

1. Establishment of a full-fledged University in the state;
2. Introduction of corrected history of Manipur upto Class X;

3. Inclusion of Manipuri language in the Schedule VIII of the Indian Constitution;
4. Shortening of religious holidays;
5. Increasing of daily allowance to prisoners;
6. Re-demarcation of the boundary of Manipur along the Indo-Burma border;
7. Deletion of outsiders from the voter list
8. Withdrawal of Armed Forces (Assam and Manipur) Special Powers Act, 1958
9. Re-introduce Inner Line Permit system to check foreigners;
10. Stop sanskritization of Manipuri language in AIR, Imphal;
11. Restore and preserve the Kangla moat;
12. Extend the Manipur Land Revenue and Land Reforms Act, 1960 to the hill areas of Manipur.
13. Deport Assam Rifles from the Kangla;
14. Lower the prices of essential commodities and bus fare;
15. Ban 10 am shows in the Cinema Halls;
16. Restore academic career disturbed by the Assam agitation;
17. Land allotment for construction of AMSU office;
18. Eviction of oddly located Kasturi Garrage in Imphal.

On the other hand, a joint meeting of AMSU led by Ng Nongyai and AMSCOC discussed the earlier demands which were submitted by AMSCOC to the Chief Minister on 15 February, 1980. The joint meeting raised a 8-point charter of demands:

1. Prevent entry of outsiders in Manipur, particularly the Nepalis;
2. Include Manipuri Language in the Schedule VIII of the Indian Constitution;
3. Convert Sadar Hills Autonomous District into a Revenue District;
4. Involve student representatives in enumeration of the ensuing 1981 Census of Manipur
5. Fix the price of all essential commodities;
6. Solve the unemployment problem;
7. Declare of first day of *Sajibu* month as public holiday for **Cheiraoba** (New Year Day);
8. Reservation in IAS and IPS for the Manipuris.

Again, the faction led by Ngangbam Nongyai, held a general body meeting on 7 March 1980. By its resolution, a memorandum containing the following demands, signed by Ng Nongyai, General Secretary was submitted to the Chief Minister.

1. A high powered judicial enquiry must be instituted into the brutal killing of a Meitei youth, arrested in connection with the 29 February incident at Paona Bazar. He was shot dead in cold blood by the soldiers of the Assam Rifles without proper confirmation of his involvement in the incident (*on the day, some unknown youths gunned down 3 jawans of Assam Rifles in broad day light)*;

2. The vulgar and indecent behaviour of the CRPF personnel and soldiers of Indian Army towards the general public while conducting body-search on the public roads must be brought to an end;

3. The influx of foreigners into Manipur must be stopped instantly. Those foreigners who were already settled in Manipur must be expelled to their respective homelands.

On 16 March, a joint meeting of the AMSU faction led by Ng Nongyai and AMSCOC was held at Johnstone Higher Secondary School, Imphal, with Mr N C Achouba, Ex-Publicity Secretary, AMSU, in the Chair. The following students were declared elected uncontested as Office bearers of AMSU for the year 1980-81:

1.	L Dilip Meetei	President
2.	S Dinamani Singh	Vice-President
3.	Y Priyokumar Singh	General Secretary
4.	Ms R K Sanajaobi Devi	Asst., General Secretary
5.	L Lukhoi	Finance Secretary.

AMSU (Dilip faction) and AMSCOC, hereinafter referred to as the AMSU-AMSCOC combine, began organising various demonstrations in Imphal area carrying festoons that read "All Manipur Students Co-ordinating Committee and AMSU"; and shouted slogans "Expel Outsiders/Aliens from Manipur", "Go back Foreigners", "Resign Kishor Thapa, MLA" etc. As a part of the continuing agitation, the combine issued a leaflet in Manipuri under the caption "Foreigners should be expelled from Manipur". The leaflet spelt out its reasons for demanding the expulsion of foreigners.

It also urged the general public to come forward in support of the students. The students went to the extent of shouting slogans and distributing pamphlets even inside the State Legislative Assembly Hall on 18 March 1980. Six students were arrested by the security personnel.

It is worthwhile mentioning that, both the AMSU factions adopted a number of methods in highlighting the issue. These include distribution of leaflets, pamphlets and booklets. These propaganda literature expressed strong fear of demographic disequilibrium in the state thereby resulting in natives being outnumbered by the outsiders. They also organised a number of public meetings and demonstrations; boycotted classes and examinations. The then student leaders disclosed to the author that both the factions of the AMSU were strongly and genuinely alarmed by a fear of losing Manipur to the foreigners.

It was interesting to note that the leaflets circulated by the AMSU(Dilip) and AMSCOC combine uses 'Meetei' while AMSU(Khelen) uses 'Meitei'. There was a long debate charged with emotion and sentiment over the ethnonyme (majority use the word 'Meitei' as ethnonyme of the non-tribal Manipuris while some section of the revivalists use 'Meetei' to mean the same). But, it did not create any confusion on their political demands and action. The Manipuris had somehow became indifferent to the ethnonyme.

They also made attempts to popularise the movement and organised it even in the hill area of Manipur. On 18 March the student volunteers of AMSCOC distributed a leaflet in Kuki dialect wherein they appealed to the tribal chiefs and villagers to support their movement and also in driving out the foreigners specially the Nepalese in the state. They further appealed to the village chiefs to check the influx of Kukis from other states. Both the factions were attentive to the problems faced by both the people in the Hills and the Plains. A strong fear of **Manipur becoming a second Tripura** was sounded. The author was told by the then student leaders (M. Khelen, to cite a name) that there was a genuine fear then of being outnumbered by the foreigners.

In the hill area, a public meeting was organised jointly by the Sadar Hill Youth Union and AMSU on 2 March 1980 at Kangpokpi. Prominent tribal leaders attended the said meeting and also delivered speeches. The meeting resolved:

(i) Voting rights of Nepalis who entered Manipur after 1958 should be curtailed;

(ii) The Nepalis who had been elected either as MLA or MDC should resign;

(iii) Nepalis tenants should not be allowed to cultivate in the hill areas.

Another resolution in support of the movement of AMSU for expulsion of the foreigners was also adopted. The meeting concluded with the shouting of slogans, "Go Back Foreigners", "We demand Revenue District", "We Want Justice", "Save Manipur", "Protect Tribal Rights", "We support Students Movement" etc. The markets of Kangpokpi, Motbung, and Keithelmanbi remained closed from 6 a.m. to 6 p.m. on March 29.

The AMSU Dilip faction staged a demonstration in the Imphal market on 18 March. That day, some activists got inside the Manipur Legislative Assembly Hall and shouted anti-foreigner slogans from the Visitor's gallery.

On the other hand, the AMSU Khelen faction came up with a decision on March 25 to boycott the High School Leaving Certificate Examination 1980, commencing from 17 April to press the Government on their 18-point charter of demands. Supporters of the Khelen faction also demonstrated inside the Assembly hall on 30 March.

The AMSU-AMSCOC combine also took a similar decision to boycott the High School Leaving Certificate Examination, but later withdrew the decision in the interest of the examinees and in accordance with the Chief Minister's assurance given on 28 March to consider at least 9 demands. The Chief Minister had reportedly assured the representatives of the AMSU-AMSCOC combine, led by W. Deben (President, AMSCOC) and L. Dilip Meetei (President, AMSU) that their demands would be fulfilled as early as possible and asked them to cooperate with the Government in solving the issue.

Further, the AMSU-AMSCOC combine appealed to the student community not to spread any baseless rumour regarding the activities of the two student organisations and not to collect fund in the name of AMSU and AMSCOC, through a leaflet issued on 26 March. They said, a few individuals are illegally using the name of AMSU and AMSCOC for their own personal and financial interest during the height of the agitation.

On 31 March, the Chief Minister had informed the AMSU (Khelen) faction that 12 out of 18 demands would be fulfilled very soon. In the absence of any assurance to the remaining 6 points, [which were demarcation of Indo-Burma boundary, withdrawal of Armed Forces Special Powers Act 1958, expulsion of aliens, introduction of Inner Line Permit System, amendment of Section 158 of Manipur Land Revenue and Land Reform Act 1960, and cancellation of 10 pm Cinema Shows;], the faction decided to continue with the boycott of the High School Leaving Certificate Examination commencing on April 17. The March 26 ultimatum expressly mentioned that the Union would boycott the ensuing HSLC Examination if the Government failed to give a favourable reply to their 18 point demands within March 31.

Posters that read as "Nepalis: Unwelcome Guest", "Are we more foreigners than foreigners", "We do not recognise Kishore Thapa as MLA", "Foreigners: Go Home", "Dismiss Foreigner MLA/MDC" etc. were displayed on the roadside trees, walls, buses, trucks etc. To suppress the students' movement and proposed mass picketing to be launched with effect from April 2, the Government ordered the closure of all the educational institutions in the Central District and Sadar Hills Area from 2 April to 10 April. In retaliation to the Government move, some students went to the Education Directorate, PWD Office, Imphal Municipality Office demanding that they should also remain closed from 2nd to 10th April, 1980. Volunteers of AMSU (Dilip) visited Government offices and threatened with dire consequences to the employees and asked them to close down their offices (PWD Stores and Mechanical Division, DC, Excise, Industries and Electricity at Lamphelpat, Rural Industries Project at Porompat and Directorate of Education, Imphal. The students hijacked one truck, one jeep belonging to PWD (Stores and Mechanical Division, Chingmeirong), and one vehicle from Porompat. The students continued their agitation with snatching of keys and locking up the doors of the Government office buildings. Meanwhile, some students went to the Cinema halls to project slides of their slogans such as "Long Live AMSU", "Go Back Foreigners", "Foreigners should be expelled", "Resign Kishore Thapa", "Manipuri Language should be included in the 8th Schedule" and "AMSCOC is for the people"

Many student leaders were arrested by the Police. But, the agitation continued. A public meeting was organised by the AMSU-AMSCOC combine on 9 April at Khurai Lamlong.

In the meeting both organisations condemned the Government for arresting the students and it criticised the Government for charging the students with vehicle theft. They also highlighted the purpose of the agitation, and appealed to the gathering for support.

On 9 April, 13 representatives of the AMSU-AMSCOC combine called on the Chief Minister to discuss their demands. The Chief Minister assured the student leaders that he would fulfil all their demands except the demand for expulsion of foreigners. However, it was agreed in principle that a student delegation should be sent to Delhi to call on the Central leaders over the issue. They also assured the Chief Minister to suspend their agitation till the return of the delegation from Delhi. 12 student volunteers of the combine who had been arrested earlier were released from judicial custody on April 10.

On 11 April, eight representatives of the two organisations led by W. Deben and L. Dilip Meetei called on the Chief Minister of Manipur. They urged the Government to postpone the HSLC and other examinations till the return of their representatives from Delhi. But, they failed to reach an agreement. Inspite of the assurance, the Union sent an ultimatum signed W. Deben (President, AMSCOC) and L. Dilip Meetei (President, AMSU) that they would resume their agitation with effect from April 15 unless the Chief Minister gave a positive reply to their demand for the postponement of the ensuing HSLC Examination from 1200 hrs of April 14. The Government disagreed with their proposals. Therefore, in a meeting held on 14 April, the AMSU-AMSCOC combine adopted the following resolutions:

"1. To boycott the ensuing HSLC Examination which

will commence from April 17 as the authority concerned has not agreed to postpone the said Examination till the return of the student representatives who are proposed to be sent to New Delhi;

2. To stop all vehicular traffic and closure of all the schools and colleges from 17 April to prevent the examinees of the HSLC Examination sitting for the examination.
3. To prevent the conduct of examination of higher classes".

With it, the students continued to disturb the functioning of Government offices and public life.

Meanwhile, S. Dinamani Singh, the Vice-President of AMSU (Dilip) faction, through a hand written cyclostyled leaflet, charged the leader of the other faction M. Khelen that he had brought disunity among the students by forming another faction of AMSU. The AMSU (Khelen) faction retaliated with a press release on 15 April stating that the expulsion of foreigners had nothing to do with the holding of HSLC Examination. It expressed that foreigners issue would not be solved by disturbing the examinations in schools and colleges, etc. It also said, some former students had been instigating some young persons to create disturbances in the name of the AMSU. The Khelen faction had earlier decided to suspend their agitation programme in the interest of the examinees.

On 15 April, the Government of Manipur placed all the Examination Centres of HSLC in Central District and Sadar Hills under prohibitory orders of Section 144 Cr.P.C. with effect from April 17 to 30 to ensure holding of the examination smoothly. The prohibition order restricted the assembly of four or more persons.

At the same time, all educational institutions in the Manipur Central District and Sadar Hills had been also ordered to remain closed from April 16 to 30. Following the closure of the schools and colleges, the students could not organise any demonstration with the participation of students. They, therefore, resorted to arson. Setting Government vehicles on fire or attempts became the main activities of the Union. On the appeal of the students, all the cinema halls remain closed on 16 April after the matinee show. On the same day, the AMSU-AMSCOC combine distributed a leaflet in and around Imphal under the caption **"To save motherland is 100 times better than Examination"**. They appealed to the examinees not to sit for the said examination and warned with dire consequences in case they ignored their appeal. Still, the arson targetted at Government buildings continued.

On 17 April, some activists of the AMSU-AMSCOC combine disturbed the examination centres at different places. They snatched away admit cards and answer scripts from the examinees, threatened teachers and even kidnapped some of them. When some of them tried to disturb the conduct of the examination at Lilashing Khongnangkhong High School, a locality in northern Imphal. CRPF personnel on duty opened fire to control the agitating students. One P. Premananda alias Lukhoi, aged 18, died on the spot. N. Somorendra Singh was wounded in the firing. Irate students set fire to a moped parked inside the school campus. Next day, after the morning examination at Leiren Girls' Higher School of Nambol (a town about 16 kms. from Imphal), a group of about six students snatched the answer scripts and torched them. Manipur Rifles personnel opened fire; and in the incident one student named Huidrom Lokendra, aged 23, of Ishok village was killed. In Imphal, examination in seven centres could not be held examination due to the violent actions of the agitating students. Under the circumstances, the HSLC Examination had to be postponed *sine die*. However, a series of other violent activities continued unabated.

The Khelen faction had remained inactive during the month of April in response to the Chief Minister's assurance on 31 March. A press release circulated by Khangembam Cha Babu, General Secretary of AMSU (Khelen) however said, the double standard of R.K. Dorendra government had compelled AMSU to take up serious steps in pursuit of its nine remaining demands including the foreigner's issue.

Earlier, on 31 March, the Government of Manipur intimated to M. Khelen that the Government has unilaterally decided to fulfil 12 of their demands. The demands were:

1. Establish a full-fledged University in the State;
2. Introduce corrected history of Manipur upto Class X;
3. Include Manipuri language in the Schedule VIII of the Indian Constitution;
4. Shorten religious holidays;
5. Increase the daily allowance of prisoners;
6. Stop sanskritisation of Manipuri language in AIR Imphal;
7. Preserve and restore the Kangla moat.
8. Deport the Assam Rifles from the Kangla.

9. Lower the prices of essential commodities and bus fare.
10. Restore the academic career disturbed by the Assam agitation.
11. Land allotment for construction of AMSU office building.
12. Eviction of the oddly located Kasturi Garrage in Imphal.

The Government also said that other demands would be fulfilled or considered before 1 May 1980.

On 18 April 1980, the AMSU-AMSCOC combine sent a telegram to the Prime Minister demanding a judicial enquiry into the death of a student in the police firing on 17 April. It also demanded the postponement of the H.S.L.C. Examination until the issue of the foreign nationals is solved. It further mentioned that the students who had been non-violent so far might resort to violence due to the behaviour of the Chief Minister.

In the meantime, the State Government initiated a meeting of representatives of the different political parties and some special invitees on 10 April to discuss the burning issue. Accordingly, R.K. Dorendra Singh, the Chief Minister wrote a letter on 5 April inviting the Presidents and the General Secretaries of CPI, CPI(M), Congress (I), Congress (U), MPP, KNA, Lok Dal, Janata Party, Ireipak Leishem Party to the meeting. Special invitees included L. Dilip, W. Deben, M. Khelen, Kh. Babu, N.K. Sanajaoba, O. Bhogendro, A. Somorendra and Th. Tarunkumar. A state level committee was formed to initiate talks with the Central Government so that a solution be reached on or before 25 April. However, R.K. Dorendra went overboard and appealed to the agitating

Assam students also, to consider 1971 as the base year for identification of foreigners in Assam. Dorendra was probably thinking of political one-upmanship in the region.

The AMSU-AMSCOC combine called a three-day Manipur *Bandh* from 21 to 23 April 1980. In a leaflet issued by the Publicity Section of the combine on 20 April, it appealed to the general public to support the bandh. It also condemned the action of the Government against the students' movement such as holding of HSLC examination, killing of two persons, promulgating of Section 144 Cr.P.C. and Curfew etc. The Manipuri leaflet went under the caption "Government should not force the students to resort to violence." The bandh was however relaxed on 23 April as a homage to the matyrs of Khongjom War. Khongjom Day is observed every 23 April in memory of the heroes who fought in the Anglo-Manipuri War of 1891.

On 21 April, some students of Sadar hills area entered the office of the SDO/Kangpokpi and forcibly took away the application forms for inclusion of names in the electoral rolls of the Kangpokpi Assembly Constituency along with the draft Electoral Rolls of 1980 and set them on fire.

Meanwhile, in response to R.K. Dorendra's appeal in the newspapers, Kh. Babu, General Secretary of AMSU (Khelen) warned in a press release that it would not wait for 1 May and would start its agitation on 26 April. They insisted that 1951 should be the base year for identification of foreign nationals.

On 3 May AMSU (Khelen) came up with a cyclostyled leaflet. It appealed to the people to fight in order to safeguard the identity of the state. It charged, the influx of the foreigners is threatening the distinct identity, religion and culture of the Meiteis.

The same day, the other faction and AMSCOC submitted a written assurance to the Chief Minister saying that they would not stage picketing or disturb offices from 3 to 6 May to enable the employees of the state to draw their monthly salaries.

On 11 May, AMSU (Khelen) in a press-note expressed its unhappiness over the alleged ill treatment and assault of Manipuri students studying outside Manipur. Supporting the campaign taken up by the students and youths, AMSU (Khelen) condemned the policy of the Government against the students involved in the agitation to expel foreigners from Manipur. Again in a press-note issued on May 13, the AMSU-AMSCOC combine expressed their unhappiness over the Government press-note of 11 May which had clarified there was no truth in the rumour that the students studying outside (Delhi) had been assaulted and asked to leave Delhi on or before 15 May 1980.

Meanwhile, volunteers drawn from the Youth Fronts of various political parties got together on 13 May and formed the Youth and Student Co-ordinating Body. It included the youth fronts of Manipur Peoples Party, Ireipak Leishem Party, Manipur Pradesh Congress Committee (I), Manipur Pradesh Congress Committee (U), All India Student Federation, SPRC, National Students Union of India, All Manipur Democratic Youth League and Student Federation of India, State Committee. In a leaflet, the body appealed to AMSU and AMSCOC and the general public to help bring normalcy in the state. It also urged the Government to withdraw all the pending cases against the leaders of AMSU and AMSCOC. Appreciating the suspension of the agitation by AMSU and AMSCOC for some time, it further appealed to them to extend the suspension for some more days with a view to restore normalcy in the state of Manipur.

It also appealed to all shopkeepers to sell essential commodities at the pre-bandh rates.

A leaflet on 21 May further expressed that "For driving out the foreigners, every ways and means available to the students and youths will be explored. That will be our law. AMSU would show by action that our choice is to save our society and our cultural heritage from the hands of the foreigners"

On 6 May, a joint meeting of the AMSU(Dilip) and AMSCOC was held at Takhel Leikai Sega Road. The meeting adopted the following resolutions:-

1. That the AMSU and AMSCOC would not negotiate with the Government till their ten demands are fulfilled (The demands included (i) to ensure correct news broadcast in AIR regarding the activities of the students, (ii) Judicial enquiry into the killing of the students in the police firing, (iii) Relief to the families of the deceased students, (iv) lifting of curfew orders u/s 144 Cr. P.C. (v) Correction of incorrect statement of the Chief Ministers' broadcast over the AIR that the students had called off strike (vi) Deployment of MR, Manipur Police and Home Guards in place of the Army and CRPF, (vii) Unconditional release of arrested students, cancellation of the cases against them (viii) Withdrawal of warrants of arrest against the students, (ix) Time of preparation for negotiations with the Chief Minister, (x) Immediate opening of the educational institutions).
2. To urge the Government to stop the arrest of the

student leaders in connection with the recent communal incidents.

3. To urge the Government to withdraw curfew orders.
4. The meeting also condemned the invitation for negotiations.
5. To start picketing and disturb the Government offices, set fire on Government offices and schools as a follow up of their programme.

Later in the evening, another meeting of the AMSU-AMSCOC combine was held at the same venue with W. Deven, President of AMSCOC in the chair. The meeting decided to postpone their proposed picketing and disturbing of Government offices to 10 May with a view to facilitate the employees to draw their salaries.

On 13 May, Yengkokpam Priyokumar, General Secretary, AMSU (Dilip) submitted a memorandum to the Chief Minister of Manipur. It demanded taking over of wholesale agencies by the State Government otherwise in the hands of the non-Manipuris. It said, such a measure would help improve communal harmony. It urged the Chief Minister for immediate action in this regard.

A press release issued by the same faction alongwith AMSCOC condemned the statement of one Akali leader for comparing the communal incidents at Imphal with those of Hindu-Muslim riots in the Partition of India.

The next day on 14 May, a meeting of the AMSU-AMSCOC combine was held at Kwakeithel Heinoukhongnembi Laishram Leikai with W. Deven (President, AMSCOC) in the chair. The meeting adopted the following resolutions:-

1. To observe a protest from 16 to 31 May wearing black badges by the volunteers of the two students' organisations with the slogan as "Go back Foreigners".
2. The volunteers of the organisation shall put up black posters on the line buses, vehicles and walls of buildings and would affix black badges to the pedestrians, cyclists etc. at street corners and road junctions.
3. To conclude picketing offices on May 15.
4. To organise a mass rally of the girl students and women wearing traditional dress at Imphal.

As a follow up, the volunteers of AMSU(D)-AMSCOC combine in small groups started to put up black posters depicting map of Manipur, slogans written as "Go back foreigners" on line buses, trucks, jeeps and auto-rickshaws from the early morning of 16 May 1980. They also affixed black badges to the pedestrians and cyclists etc. at important road crossings at Imphal.

The All Naga Students Association, Manipur also condemned the State Government for its alleged failure to bring normalcy and urged the state and central Governments to make a speedy settlement of the foreigners issue with the striking students and restore harmony among all sections of people in Manipur.

On 18 May, 97 persons (many students were arrested in connection with the foreigners issue) were released unconditionally from Jail. The same day, AMSU(Dilip) distributed copies of a cyclostyled leaflet in Manipuri in red ink which contained the following demands:-

1. Immediate stop to combing operations,
2. Expulsion of the foreigners from the state,
3. Introduction of Inner-Line Permit system;
4. Withdrawal of Armed Forces Special Power Act (Assam and Manipur) 1958,
5. Deletion of Section 158 from Manipur Land Revenue and Land Reform Act 1960,
6. Restoration of Kabaw Valley to Manipur.

On 19 May, AMSU(Dilip) and AMSCOC jointly organised a silent procession with a newly formed organisation called "Nongpok Thong".

Again on 23 May, AMSU (Dilip) distributed copies of a printed leaflet in Manipuri in Imphal town area under the caption "AMSU Starts Movement". It contained the 6 new demands and one more demand that 1951 should be the base year for expulsion of the foreigners.

On the same day (23 May) some unidentified youth came to the shop of P.C. Jain, Newspaper Agent at Thangal Bazar, Imphal. They put seal marking as "Go Back Foreigners", "Introduce Inner Line Permit System", "Repeal Armed Forces Special Powers Act 1958" on the English newspapers kept for sale.

On 25 May, AMSU (Khelen) distributed copies of a printed leaflet in Manipuri. It highlights that the population of Manipur has increased more than 50% of the average all India growth rate during the last 20 years because of the influx of foreigners. These foreigners have settled on the Government Khaslands which could be (otherwise) used as paddy fields or kept reserved for our future generation.

Thus influx also resulted in the scarcity of food and price rise of essential commodities. It appealed to the State Government to check influx of the foreigners and expel those who have already settled in their state.

Meanwhile, the United Matric Students Association submitted a memorandum to the Chief Minister demanding announcement of a definite date for holding of High School Leaving Certificate Examination and other examinations. It also demanded to enquire into the killing of students in the Police firing.

The AMSU-AMSCOC combine issued a press-note expressing their unhappiness over the reopening of classes in Regional Medical College from 2 June. It demanded the cessation of classes immediately till June 15, 1980. They also issued a booklet under the title **"Facts and Figures: Influx of foreigners in Manipur"**. It contained the following demands:-

a. Settlement of the question of foreigners on the basis of appropriate provisions of the constitution of India and relevant Acts.

b. Foreigners must be identified on the basis of 1951 Census.

c. Detection and deportation of foreigners should be jointly implemented by the Government of India and Manipur.

d. All the moveable and immoveable properties of those declared foreigners must be vested in the Government of Manipur.

e. Indian citizens giving either direct or indirect protection to the foreigners should be punished. Foreigners in Manipur with citizenship certificates from West Bengal, Tripura and any other state should be sent back to those states and outsider influx into Manipur should be prevented under a specially enacted legislation.

f. Distinct identity and ethnic composition of Manipur Nation and their nationalities in the North-East Region should be preserved and the right of the original inhabitants of the region in respect of employment, settlement of land etc. be promoted under specially enacted constitutional provisions.

g. The National Register of Citizens (1951) should be brought upto date by enacting the names of all the original inhabitants of Manipur and deleting the names of all the foreigners in the state.

h. Electoral Rolls should be prepared on the basis of the National Register of Citizens up-to-date, and

i. Birth and death registration should be made obligatory for all the original inhabitants of Manipur.

On 3 June an exclusive meeting of AMSU (Khelen) was held at the residence of M. Khelen, President, AMSU. The meeting decided to urge the Government to review the memorandum drafted by the political leaders jointly for submission to the Prime Minister regarding the foreigners issue etc. on the ground that the memorandum did not mention the base year and that public opinion was not taken into consideration before drafting the memorandum. It also condemned the Government's frequent promulgation of curfew in Manipur.

On 7 June, the AMSU-AMSCOC combine sent a telegram to the Prime Minister of India. It lodged a protest against the memorandum submitted by the representatives of all political parties of Manipur to the Prime Minister. It stated that, the memorandum did not mention the base year for the expulsion of the foreigners and that no one from AMSU and AMSCOC was consulted before drafting the memorandum.

The combine distributed a pamphlet in Manipuri in Imphal and other parts of Manipur announcing the observance of Black Day on 13 June. It contained among other things the following slogans.

1. Foreigners should not acquire any property.
2. Go back Foreigners, Good bye foreigners.
3. Let us show the world that the North-East region is one.
4. Long live 'North-East Region Students Union'.
5. Long live seven sisters unity.

On 13 June, 'Black Day' was observed by taking out a procession in Imphal. A public meeting was also held at the Imphal Pologround.

The faction led by M. Khelen also started a slogan campaign from 13 June, after being inactive for sometime. The slogans painted in Red on jeeps include among others:

1. Go Back Foreigners.
2. Introduce Inner Line Permit.
3. Base Year 1951.

The faction also organised a torch rally on 23 June. The rally which started from the Palace Compound carried torches, red festoons and white flags. Seven persons dressed in black took the lead.

The government announced the reopening of Schools and colleges from 1 July after the Summer vacation. However no classes could be conducted in many of the schools and colleges in Imphal area, as many of school buildings and furniture were damaged during the agitations. School buildings in some areas were used as relief camps for the refugees and some others were occupied by the CRPF.

As a protest the students did not attend classes, but on different reasons. Such as:

1. Lilasing Khongnangkhong High School - Non-repairing of school building
2. Ananda Singh Academy - Non-repairing of school building
3. Tombisana High School - Demanding adequate furniture
4. Bengali High School - Demanding evacuation of the refugees
5. Churachand Higher Secondary School - Demanding removal of CRPF personnel from the school

The AMSU-AMSCOC combine observed "Mass Consciousness Day" from 1 to 7 July. AMSU (Dilip) and AMSCOC were approached by the Government of Manipur for negotiations at that time. They were demanding fulfilment of some pre-conditions which were rather new demands. They were (1) to ensure correct broadcast of student activities in AIR, Imphal; (2) judicial enquiry into the killing of the students in the police firing; (3) compensation to the families of the deceased students; (4) withdrawal of curfew; (5) correction of wrong statement of Chief Minister in AIR, Imphal that students had called off the strike; (6) deployment of Manipur Riffles, Manipur Police and Home Guards in place of the Army and CRPF; (7) unconditional release of the arrested students and cancellation of the cases against them; (8) withdrawal of warrants of arrest against the students; (9) time of preparation for negotiations with the Chief Minister; (10) immediate opening of the educational institutions.

The other faction led by Khelen was adverse to discuss the issue with the Chief Minister only. They demanded a 'national' decision to solve the problem permanently. And it also condemned the police act of firing on the students on 17 April and took a resolution to demand a judicial enquiry into the police firing on 20 April. It may be mentioned here that the students were killed during the strike of the AMSU-AMSCOC combine.

On 17 July, they went to the Novelty Press, Paona Bazar and damaged the electoral rolls. Again on 19 July they snatched the printed copies of electoral rolls and some original copies from the National Press, Paona Bazar.

On 18 July, volunteers of the AMSU-AMSCOC combine attacked the office of the Principal, I.T.I., Takyel for conducting examinations. They set fire to some furniture inside the office of the Principal causing damage to the furniture and files. Earlier on 11 July, the Gauhati Manipuri Students' Association supporting the demands of AMSU and AMSCOC issued a press-note under the caption **"No examination in Manipur till the foreigners issue is settled"**. It appealed to the students community not to sit for any examination and further it added that "the issue for expulsion of foreigners is more important than the examination".

By the end of July, the State Government was successful in initiating negotiation with the AMSU-AMSCOC combine. On 22 July, Chief Minister R.K. Dorendra met Y. Priyokumar, General Secretary of AMSU (Dilip) and W. Deben Singh, President, AMSCOC and signed an agreement at 3.00 p.m. the same day, in the Chief Minister's office chamber.

The Chief Minister and the Minister of State for Sports M. Kumar Singh discussed with the representatives of the AMSU and the AMSCOC at 3.00 p.m. to-day, the 22 July, 1980 for finding a solution to the 'Foreigners' Issue. It was agreed that the Government shall start processing of identification of the foreigners with the co-operation of the representatives of the AMSU and AMSCOC from the 1 August 1980. The Government and the representatives of the students agreed to identify the foreigners under the Constitution and the law. The details of the student representatives shall be finalised on or before the 5 August, 1980. The representatives of AMSU and AMSCOC have agreed to suspend their agitation on 'Foreigners' issue till the 5 of August, 1980. "The Agreement was signed by R.K. Dorendra Singh, Chief Minister of Manipur with Y. Priyokumar Singh, Secretary General of AMSU and W. Deben Singh, President of AMSCOC.

Following the agreement, the programmes of picketing and Bandh scheduled to start on 23 July was dropped. The agitation programme was decided in a joint meeting attended by 120 representatives of Branch offices, wings and office bearers at Imphal College on 11 July.

On 28 July, the AMSU-AMCOC combine had issued a

four page printed hand bill in Manipuri under the caption "Important points on foreigners issue". It discussed inter alia about making 1951 as the base year for identification of foreigners and appealed for implementation of the Manipur Merger Agreement Act 1949 with regard to the protection of the interests of the Manipuris for appointment the in All India services etc.

On the other hand, the other AMSU faction led by Khelen had diverted its attention to hoarding of essential commodities by big businessmen. They forcibly seized essential commodities from the godowns and distributed the same to the public free of cost. In a booklet circulated on 27 August 1980, N. Budha Meitei, Editor General of AMSU (Khelen) justified its action as "During the agitation for expulsion of foreigners, the colonial puppet ministry of R.K. Dorendra imposed curfew *indefinitely* to protect the foreigners thereby causing serious repercussions to the society. No Manipuri was allowed to go out, not even to buy essential commodities. On the other hand the State Government refuse to look into the stock of comodities, kept secretly by the **Mayang** merchants. In fact, they were dancing to the tune of these Mayangs". Thus, they began raiding the godowns. In the course of such activities, two students namely Konsam Imoba, aged 18 of Khagempalli and Thokchom Naba, aged 18 of Nganapi Thong drowned in the Imphal River while trying to escape from a police patrol on 30 April 1980.

AMSU (Khelen) did not accept the Government's proposals as the Government did not agree to 1951 as the base year for identification of foreigners and the State Government refuse to invite the Central Government as a party to the 'proposed' negotiations.

On 6 August three student representatives, L. Dilip (AMSU), Home (AMSCOC) and R.K. Priyobarta, Advisor (AMSCOC) called on the Chief Minister. They discussed the steps to be taken up by the Government over the identification and expulsion of foreigners. An agreement was also said to have been reached between the student representatives and the Chief Minister in this regard. The Chief Minister also assured the withdrawal of arrest warrants pending against the students for their involvement in the agitation on foreigners issue and also release of the remaining students.

On 10 August again, representatives of AMSU and AMSCOC called on the Chief Minister R.K. Dorendra. As the Chief Minister was indisposed, the students were asked to discuss the issue with the Deputy Chief Minister Rishang Keishing. Accordingly the students called on the Deputy Chief Minister at his bungalow office. However no talks could be held between the students and the Dy. C.M. There was disagreement on the nature of the talks. The students insisted that the discussion should be on the lines of agreement reached between them and the Chief Minister. The Dy. C.M. wanted to have a preliminary talk on the issue. The students refused any further discussion and left the place.

On 11 August, AMSU and AMSCOC decided in a meeting to call back Manipuri students reading outside Manipur as soon as possible to avoid any backlash in the wake of the anti-foreigners agitation. The meeting was attended by Joynath Sharma (Chief Convenor, AASU), Bharat Nath (Asst. Gen. Secy., AASU) and W. Deven in the chair.

On 12 August, a joint meeting of student representatives of different communities, organised by AMSU and AMSCOC was held at D.M. College of Arts and Commerce, with L. Dilip Meetei (President, AMSU) in the chair. It discussed on how to bring mutual cooperation amongst the different communities in the students movement. The meeting was adjourned *sine-dine* as representatives from many communities did not turn up.

In the second week of August 1980 a meeting of both sections of AMSU was held at the premises of Manipur Dramatic Union Hall, Yaiskul. It discussed the unification of the two groups, but no settlement could be reached.

The AMSU-AMSCOC combine called Manipur Bandh on 15 August. At Thoubal, the National Flag at the office of the Sub Divisional Officer, Thoubal was pulled down and tored by student activists. A jeep (NLK-9157) belonging to the Irrigation and Flood Control Department was hijacked and set on fire at Top village. Six students including Yengkokpam Priyokumar, General Secretary of AMSU was arrested in this connection. Later the same day, some unknown youths pulled down the National Flag at the Congress Bhavan Imphal. Another Flag at Kanglatongbi was also pulled down and carried away by unknown students. A truck (NLK-4997 of Assam Bengal Carrier) was also set on fire at Heingang.

In a press-note issued by the AMSU-AMSCOC combine, it denied the charge of the General Secretary of Congress (U) that the students have dishonoured the National Flag. It clarified that AMSU and AMSCOC should not be held responsible for the incident just because it happened on the day of Manipur Bandh called by the two organisations. It clarified that the AMSU and AMSCOC respects the National flag and the Indian Constitution.

In another press-note the student combine demanded postponement of census operations being started from 1 September. It mentioned that any census made before the foreigners issue is settled would make things more complicated.

On 23 August, the AMSU-AMSCOC combine appealed to the teachers-in-charge and Finance Secretaries of the students unions in all schools and colleges to suspend all the external educational excursions. It further mentioned that the two organisations should not be held responsible for any consequences, if they disregard the appeal.

FINAL NEGOTIATIONS AND AFTERMATH

AMSU (Khelen) refused to negotiate on the foreigners' issue with the Government unless the base year is 1951 and also the Central Government a party to such a negotiation. The AMSU-AMSCOC combine, however, negotiated with the representatives of the Government of Manipur. They entered into the final round of negotiations on 5 August 1980. An agreement was signed on 5 August 1980 by L. Dilip Meetei, President of AMSU (Dilip), W. Deven Singh, President of AMSCOC, R.K. Dorendra, Chief Minister, Government of Manipur and M. Kumar Singh, State Minister (Public Health Engineering and Sports) Government of Manipur. The Government of Manipur agreed,

> (i) to start the process of identification and detection of foreigners from 1 August 1980 with the co-operation of AMSU and AMSCOC defining the question of **foreigner** as per the Constitution and the law of India ; (ii) to identify foreigners from this date of the enforcement of the Constitution of India i.e. from 26 January 1950 while giving due attention to the electoral rolls of different

years for comparison starting from 1948 ; (iii) to identify foreigners on the basis of the census report (1951) and the National Register of Citizens (1951) and Village directory (1951) ; (iv) to expel unlawful settlers from the K.K.Reserve areas, Protected Areas, Khas lands and other reserve areas starting from 7 August 1980 and to take up aforestration programme in the areas so evicted as such areas are normally denuded; (v) to send back foreigners in Manipur with citizenship certificate from West Bengal, Tripura and any other states should be sent back to the state concerned to prevent such infiltration under specially enacted legislation ; (vi) to strengthen check posts at Imphal Dimapur Road, Jiribam, Moreh, Tipaimukh, Airport (Imphal), etc. to restrict the entry of foreigners, OSDs to be posted at various places, i.e. Mao, Karong, Jiribam, Moreh, Tipaimukh and Airport, etc. and request to check the Manipur bound passengers ; (vii) to hold a joint meeting of the Deputy Commissioners and Chairman of District Councils with the representatives of AMSU and AMSCOC on August 1980 in the Office chamber of C.M. for necessary tasks for identification and detection of foreigners ; (viii) to pursue to the Government of India jointly for the inclusion of Manipuri language in the Eighth Schedule of the Indian Constitution ; (ix) to take into confidence the people in the central district and reach a consensus at the time of formation of Sadar hills district and reach a consensus at the time of formation of Sadar hills district; (x) to propose the formation of a Committee on Essential Commodities to fix the price for much items as oil, rice, edible oils, cotton yarn and other materials which are highly needed for daily life ; (xi) to reserve in all kinds of jobs for Manipuris in the jobs orientation programme and also give land loans for small scale industries to unemployed (educated and uneducated) youths to set up industries which were agreed upon by the central Government with immediate effect, such as industries of glucose and starch factory, sugar factory, mini-cement plant and also to purchase for setting up a pulp and paper industry at Jiribam and etc. (xii) 'The Government shall also give all chances, facilities of jobs which can be done by the local people in the Government and Semi-Government Schemes'; (xiii) to insert a specific subsection in the Manipur Land Reforms and Land Revenue Act, 1960 (under section (158) a preventive measure to check the transfer of immovable properties from Manipuri to non-Manipuri in the Central District and also to bring the matter to the notice of the Cabinet: (xiv) to review the system of reservation in service/promotion present by enjoyed by scheduled castes and schedule tribes in the Cabinet meeting with a view to cancel the existing reservation ; (xv) to declare Manipuri as backward class equivalent to scheduled caste in legal and constitutional sense with restrospective effect from the date of merger of the state of Manipur to the Union Government ; (xvi) to deliberate budgeting provisions on the basis of needs ; (xvii) further it was also agreed that agitation programmes would depend upon the progress of implementation of negotiated terms, strongly the provisions of the agreement were not to be public immediately.

In the agreement, slight factual mistakes were seen such as the 'reservation' mentioned in the Article VIII (3) of the Merger Agreement of 1949 was not on the basis of 'backwardness'. The attempt to declare the Meitei as a 'schedule caste' in 1982, faced opposition from various sections of the population.

Soon after, the combine started blaming the State Government that it has dishonoured the Agreement and even went to the extent of calling a *Bandh* on 15 August, the Independence Day of India. This was followed by violent actions in different parts of the state. The student leaders felt deceived by the Government of Manipur.

On 27 August, a three-day conference was organised by the combine at the Government Polytechnic, Takyel, Imphal. Maharaja Kumar Priyorbarta, the ex-Chief Minister of Manipur presided over the function. It adopted the following resolutions:

a. That the concerned authority be pressurized for the detection and deportation of foreigners from Manipur;

b. That a memorandum be sent to the Prime Minister regarding the foreign nationals issue;

c. That the AMSU and AMSCOC be empowered to take up necessary steps regarding the foreign nationals issue.

That day, both the factions observed Hunger Marchers Day in their ways. In a function, leaders of AMSU(D) paid homage to the "1965 Hunger Marchers" in the morning. The gathering was dominated by the angry students' condemning the "irresponsible" Government. Meanwhile, the AMSU (Khelen) faction took out a rally from the premises of Maharaja Bodhachandra College, Imphal at about 7.15 pm and proceeded towards the AMSU monument at Pishum passing through Sanjenthong bridge and Indo-Burma Road. They also carried coffins symbolically representing the 'death in police brutality'. As the procession approached the gate of 1st Manipur Rifles, police opened fired several rounds to stop them. Altogether 13 student leaders were arrested. But after about 30 minutes, the procession was reorganised and further taken upto Pishum. The volunteers of AMSU (Khelen) had earlier disturbed the offices of Agriculture Department, Forest Department, Veterinary and Animal Husbandry Department, Motor Vehicle Department, P W D, Electricity Department, Inspectors of

School (Zone I) and Education Department in the morning.

On 29 August, AMSU (Khelen) organized a rally of about 500 persons demanding the release of students arrested on 27 August alongwith with its earlier demands to make 1951 as the base year for deportation of foreigners; withdrawal of Armed Forces (Assam and Manipur) Special Powers Act, 1958; Judicial enquiry in the police excesses on 27 August 1980; and deletion of Section 158 of Manipur Land Reforms and Land Revenue Act of 1960. At the same time, AMSU (Khelen) started a new phase of movement from 1 September, 1980 in protest against the steps taken up by the Government to identify the foreigners before finalizing the base year. The faction set on fire 3 Government vehicles. They decided to continue their agitation till the Government accepts 1951 as the base year.

Announcing the observance of **"Meetop Tanba Hak'chin Numit"** (Anti-Foreigners Day), the faction called a total Manipur *Bandh* on 3 September. In a circular issued 1 September in connection with the *Bandh,* the Publicity Section of the faction announced that it had started sabotage of the Government machineries: *the Government has reportedly started identifying foreigners without determining the base year, AMSU demands that 1951 should be the base year ... On the foreigners' issue, there is no agreement between AMSU and the Government of Manipur".* Altogether 33 students were arrested, but were released the next day. At the same time, AMSU (Khelen) strongly condemned the arrest of students who demanded the expulsion of foreigners from Manipur. It also said that the movement on such a national issue could not be suppressed by repressive measures. It appealed the Government to stop arresting the students and immediate release of all the arrested students.

Meanwhile, AMSU (Dilip) and AMSCOC held a joint meeting on 10 September at the premises of Churachand Higher Secondary School, Imphal. Kh Jibon Singh, Advisor AMSCOC, in his speech expressed a desire that examination should be held as early as possible so that the students might not lose their academic year but the other leaders did not share his view. The joint meeting decided, among others, to set certain conditions for holding examination. They were:

a. Settlement between the students and the Government over the foreigners' issue;
b. Opening of Manipur University;
c. Establishment of Engineering College;
d. Conversion of L M S Law College to a Government college;
e. Lifting of Disturbed Area Act; and
f. Opening of examination centres for competitive examinations like IAS, IPS in Manipur.

The faction also invited leaders of political parties to a joint meeting. Objections and opinions on the Foreigner Issue of the political parties were sought. The joint meeting of the representatives of the political parties and student leaders of the AMSU-AMSCOC combine was held on 28 September, 1980 at the premises of Churachand Higher Secondary School, Imphal. W Deben Meitei presided over the meeting. At the meeting, Hemam Nilamani Singh, President, Indian National Congress (I) was in favour of making 1971 as the base year for detection of the foreigners and urged for an amicable settlement with the Government over the issue. Th Joykumar Singh of Ireipak Leishem Party stated that there should be no question of base year and that all foreigners should be detected and deported without fixing any base year. Oinam Joy Singh, Convenor, People's Democratic Front, assured that he would raise the issue of foreigners in the State Assembly. Regarding the holding of the examinations, he was of the opinion that it was not possible to hold examinations in the present situation. H Indusekhar Sharma of the Manipur Peoples Party supported the movement of the combine. J F Rothangliana, President of Kuki National Assembly expressed his opinion that 1951 should be the base year. The meeting decided to call another meeting of the political leaders and students shortly and decided to form a Committee of all political parties to work jointly over the detection and deportation of the foreigners, holding of examinations and checking of price rise in Manipur.

Inspite of the consultations, the combine started organising processions and other activities afresh after a brief silence. They took out a procession of students on 24 September. They also announced on 19 October, that they would call a Manipur *Bandh* on 22 October to coincide with the rescheduled High School Leaving Certificate Examination. The *Bandh* was, however, cancelled in the last hours of 21 October, after an agreement was reached between their representatives and the Chief Minister, Manipur. They agreed to complete i) the identification of the foreigners in all the districts by all the DCs except those cases which would not be resolved because of unavoidable circumstances; ii) the Chief Minister further agreed that the examination would be held on the 22 October 1980 positively because of grievances of the students. However, some students strongly objected to the examination as floods had occurred in the state. This section of the students, they said should be allowed to appear in the supplementary examination which the Government has agreed to hold for the students coming from the flood affected areas but to appear only once.

As a result of this agreement, the leaders of the the AMSU-AMSCOC combine agreed to withdraw the call for *Manipur Bandh* on the 22 October and agreed to cooperate in the peaceful conduct of the examination as scheduled on the 22 October 1980. The agreement was signed by L Dilip Meetei, President of AMSU and RK Dorendro Singh, Chief Minister of Manipur with A Ibopishak Singh, PS to the Chief Minister as the witness. The Chief Minister appreciated the initiatives taken by the General Secretary of the All Manipur Secondary Teachers' Association and the All Manipur Teachers' Co-ordinating Committee, for faciliatating the compromise between the leaders of the AMSU-AMSCOC combine and the Government.

Prior to the agreement, there was a communication between the AMSU-AMSCOC combine and the Government. On 19 October, the combine sent a reminder at about noon with regard to the identification of foreigners, and the HSLC Examination. The Chief Minister also replied on the same day. In his reply, the Chief Minister asked the combine to "release a pressnote so that there may not be any confusion or doubt in the minds of the examinees and guardians." The rescheduling of the Examination was initiated by the Education Minister on 3 October in a joint meeting of representatives of both factions of AMSU, AMSCOC alongwith the Secretary, Board of Secondary Education Manipur, Director of Education and the Vice Chancellor of Manipur University. Even after the *Manipur Bandh* was called off by the AMSU-AMSCOC combine, the Education Minister sought for a meeting. From the beginning, AMSU (Khelen) had given the green signal to the said examination "in the interest of the examinees".

The foreigners agitation took a dramatic turn when a group of 7 leaders of the combine went to Delhi on 27 October to submit a memorandum to the Prime Minister of India. The team consisted of W Deben, President of AMSCOC, Y Priyokumar, General Secretary of AMSU (Dilip), Sanajaobi Devi, R K Priyobarta, M Jotin and P. Ashok. Meanwhile on 4 November, other leaders including L Dilip Meetei, President of AMSU, T Shyamananda @ Lambu, Finance Secretary of AMSCOC, assisted by Potsangbam Asok Singh Advocate, called on the Union Finance Minister R Venkataraman at the Imphal Raj Bhavan regarding their demands for expulsion of Foreigners, job facilities, more electric power etc. They also urged to the Union Minister to stop harassment and torture by the Army and to withdraw Armed Forces (Assam and Manipur) Special Powers Act of 1958. The Minister assured that he would give special consideration for giving appointment to the Manipuris in the Banks, Life Insurance Corporation, and other fields under his Ministry.

On 15 November, a press conference was organized by the combine. W Deben Meitei, President of AMSCOC, L Dilip Meetei, President of AMSU, RK Priyobarta Singh, Advisor of AMSU briefed the press. The points were:

1. That the 3 student leaders submitted their memorandum on October 31 to the office of the Prime Minister and they could meet the Prime Minister on November 3 for a duration of two minutes only. The Prime Minister assured them of a solution;
2. That on 4 November, the three leaders called on the Home Minister who asked the students delegation to complete the identification of the foreigners as soon as possible and that he would

be visiting Imphal in the month of December, 1980 after finalizing the programme with the Chief Minister of Manipur.

3. The students did not disturb the reschedule HSLC examination.
4. 50 and 2120 Nepalis had been identified so far as foreigners in Tengnoupal and South Districts respectively.

The combine also started a relay hunger strike from 24 November till 1 December and called a *Jiribam Bandh* on 1 December. In the meantime, they sent an ultimatum to the Prime Minister through the Chief Minister on 4 December that their demand should be fulfilled within 10 December 1980. At last, they also tried to seek help from different political parties like the Ireipak Leisem Party, the Manipur Peoples Party and the Bhartiya Janata Party, Manipur Pradesh.

Indefinite hunger strike started from 12 January culminating in the boycott of Republic Day Celebrations alongwith a Bandh. The decision of the boycott was taken on 21 January, 1981. On 30 January, representatives of AMSU (Dilip) called on the Education Minister and urged for release of the arrested hunger strikers before the commencement of Pre-University Course Examination to be held on 16 February, 1981.

On 5 February, an agreement was signed by the Education Minister Th. Devendro Singh, L Dilip Meetei, President of AMSU and Kh Loken Singh, Assistant General Secretary of AMSCOC. Under the agreement, all the students arrested in connection with the hunger strike on foreign nationals issue are to be released while the student representatives agreed to co-operate with the State Government in peaceful conduct of the ensuing Pre-University and other examinations being conducted by the Manipur University.

Although the issue of foreigners was not able to bring a positive outcome in the total political system inspite of the various agreements, the movement did raised the level of political consciousness among the students and the general people. The earnest desire for survival and a life with dignity for the Manipuris was highlighted. During the agitation, different means were employed by the students for attainment of their goals. Some of the damaged properties are listed below:

Date	*Place*	*Nature*
1980		
5 April	Imphal	4 Govt vehicles hijacked; recovered the same day
16 April	Kwakeithel	Set fire to a bus of Indian Airlines (WBS 6131)
		Khwai Bazar Attempt to set fire a FCS jeep(MNG 515)
		Chingamathak Set fire a car of General Manager, MSRTC
17 April	Thangmeiband	A luna moped (MNS2626) damaged
18 April	Nambol	Set fire to exam papers
		Chingamathak Set fire one jeep of Industry Deptt, Ukhrul(MNG 592)
		Porompat Office of Inspector of Zone II set on fire
19 April	Mayai Koibi	Set fire a jeep (MNS 6769) of Horticulture Deptt
12 July	Imphal	Threat to 4 presses for printing voter lists

17 July	Imphal	Snatching electoral rolls from Friends Industrial Press
18 July	Takyel	Attempt to set fire the ITI building
	Imphal	Pushed the jeep of District Industry Centre (MNG 546) in the Nambul River
15 August	Top Leikai	Set a jeep of IFCD on fire (NLK 9157)
	Imphal	Attempt to set fire a water tanker of AR (MNG 589)
	Heingang	Set a Tata truck of Assam Bengal Carrier
		(NLK 4997) on fire
	Thoubal	National Flag pulled down
	Kanglatongbi	National Flag pulled down
5 Sept	Porompat	Set fire a jeep of Vety. Deptt (MNG 680) (686)
19 Oct	Imphal	Set fire the furniture of Oriental College, Imphal
		College, Kebol Girls H/S, Manipur College, and Ch Iboyaima College
20 Oct	Imphal	Attempt to set fire Haobam Marak H/S
1981		
24 Jan	Kwakeithel	Set fire Mini Bus(MNS 5037) of Welfare Bureau
		Keisampat Set fire a jeep of Agri Dept(MNG 743)
25 Jan	Imphal	Set Tabluex of Electricity, Manipur Central Jail on fire; they were prepared for **Republic Day**
26 January		Imphal Set a motor cycle on fire.

The Reconciliation

On 17 July 1981, a meeting was held at the office of the Students' Union, Churachand Higher Secondary School with L Dilip, President of AMSU in the chair. It discussed the alleged statement of Radhabinod Koijam, Power Minister made in the floor of the Assembly on 16 July that there are no foreigners in the electoral rolls and that there was no influx of foreigners in Manipur. The meeting condemned the statement given by the Power Minister and resolved to take up appropriate action if the Minister did not tender an apology on this matter immediately.

On 22 August, the AMSU-AMSCOC combine clarified through a press note which said, they had reached an agreement with RK Dorendro Singh, Chief Minister in the month of July 1980 for the detection of foreigners. They also expressed that if the Power Minister were keen to detect the foreigners in Manipur from the electoral rolls, they would be able to point out the names of the foreigners.

By the end of the long agitation, the two AMSU factions had come closer. Mr. E. Yaima Singh, the Director of Education Dept, Government of Manipur, called a joint meeting of the Principals of 18 Colleges and 10 student leaders. There, both the factions had an open discussion over the elections to the student unions of colleges for the 1980-81 session. In the meeting, both L Dilip Meetei and M Khelen were also present. Two resolutions were taken unanimously "in view of the academic abnormal situation in 1980-81, they are

1. It was agreed that Elections to the students' Union of 80-81 session will be held after the Pre-University Examination, 1981 preferably within the first week of October, 1981;

2. It was also agreed that Pre-University IInd year and Degree IInd year students who are to appear at the University Final examinations after few days be not allowed to contest the students' Union election as they may not be in a position to fully serve the interests of the students who are at present studying in the colleges. Further, it was agreed that the voting right in the said election be given to the IInd year students (PU and Degree) to enable those who like to participate in the election to exercise their voting rights.

After the said elections in different colleges, a new set of student representatives came into the student politics. Some progressive new student leaders came to a conclusion that M Khelen and L Dilip should be asked to hold a common election to AMSU so that the Union would no longer suffer woes of factionalism. A meeting of such new student leaders was held on 31 December 1981 with Soibam Tejamani, the newly elected General Secretary of Oriental College Students' Union in the chair. The meeting was attended by the Presidents of both the factions. It took three resolutions which was signed by the presidents of both AMSU factions and the meeting President Soibam Tejamani. The resolutions are:

1. In order to unite the two factions of AMSU, it is agreed to hold a common election (to the office bearers of AMSU);
2. There will be no other election to AMSU;
3. There shall be representatives of both the factions to the Election Committee. *(It is free translation from one in Manipuri).*

Thereafter, a common Election Committee of AMSU was formed with the members from both the factions. The members were L Dilip Meetei (Chairman), M Khelen (Returning Officer), Kh Babu Meitei (Convenor), Y Priyokumar (Member), Kh Loken (Member) and L. Lukhoi (Member). The common election was held on 10 January 1982 and Ng Nongyai was elected as the President of the unified AMSU in the post foreigners issue. The other members elected to the Executive Council were K. Krishnachandra, K Surjit, N Noren, T Chanu Tondon, Bijoy Kangjam, Krishnakumar Kongjengbam, Promila Devi and Irom Roshan. They were declared elected without any contest. Before closing this chapter, it is necessary as the author feels, to look at the frequency of student overt activities of 1980-81 in comparison with that of 1981-82.

	Type of Activity	*1980-81*	*1981-82*
1.	Procession/Demonstration/Rally	31	10
2.	Class Boycott	30	30
3.	Relay Hunger Strike	3	0
4.	Indefinite Hunger Strike	2	1
5.	Disturbance to Govt establishments including school	28	4
6.	Picketing	4	0
7.	**Bandh**	6	1
8.	Hijacking Govt vehicles	3	0
9.	Mischief by fire	19	13

6

AMSU AND INTEREST ACCUMULATION FOR THE LANGUAGE ISSUE

The extended anti-foreigner agitation came to an end without much achievement. The agreement also could not be implemented for various reasons. In fact, inherent defects in the agreement itself were largely responsible for its non-implementation. For example, the agreement did not have a binding on the Central Government; it also did not empower the Deputy Commisssioners to constitute a team for detection of foreigners. On the part of AMSU, in Phase IV it could no longer mobilize the general people as they were fed up with the monotonous statistics of foreigners and invisible political outcome of the agitation which had spoiled one academic year of the students. Besides, there were heavy losses in public property.

After the Foreigners issue, AMSU was not able to take up other issues of the same magnitude. Its time was occupied by routine matters. Its activity ranges from giving pressure for re-opening of schools affected by the teachers' strikes to digging up of the old Kangla moat at Pureilomba area or so.

During the term of President Ng. Nongyai (1978-79),

AMSU came closer to NERSU (North Eastern Region Students' Union). He sent a letter dated 21 January 1983 to the then Prime Minister of India to release Jatin Mali and Hiten Goswami unconditionally who were arrested by Assam Police in Gauhati on 5 January 1983 under the National Security Act. It even called for a complete **class boycott** on 14 February as a protest against the holding of elections in Assam. A NERSU circulation dated 30 January said, *In Assam, the agitating parties have been boycotting the general elections since 1980. This time, the Assam Government has forcefully imposing assembly as well as parliamentary elections that shall be starting from the 14th February 1983 without settlement of foreigners issue in the state*. The decision of the class boycott was taken by a joint urgent meeting of representatives of AMSU and Jatin Mali, Advisor to NERSU on 29 January in Imphal.

Again, in a joint meeting of the representatives of AMSU and Manipur University Students' Council on 8 February 1983 at 11 a.m. the point was further discussed. The meeting resolved (1) to condemn the general elections of Assam, (2) to solve the foreigners' issue of the entire North East Region; (3) Repeal of the Armed Forces (Assam and Manipur) Special Powers Act 1958 and protection of human rights in the states etc. (4) Central Government should solve the foreigners' issue in Manipur before the general election, (5) Class boycott on 14 February 1983. This shows the political outlook and its change among the leaders of the students in the region because each state student body could not give due pressure alone on the Central Government.

Another routine work of **Realization Day** on 17 April of every year was added in 1981 to remember the **Anti-Foreigner Movement** and to pay homage to the students who were killed on 17 and 18 April 1980. The names of

Konsam Imoba and Thokchom Naba who died in the course of anti-foreigners' agitation are not mentioned.

On 5 October, AMSU released a press-note. It says that *Our identity will vanish from the globe as the same will not be able to protect / save itself from the continuous influx of foreigners.* It also criticised the Chief Minister for his speech in the Assembly that foreigners issue is an issue in name only. It stated that the Chief Minister has closed his eyes to the foreigners who are residing in Jiribam, Serou, Khoidum, Lamjao Saiton, Ngamukon, Kanglatongbi, Mantripukhri etc.etc. It claimed that there are 1,42,023 foreigners according to 1971 Census and the population of only the Nepalis exceeded 84,212. It forecast that one day the fate of the Assamese will be fall on us surely.

AMSU also started observing the signing of Manipur Merger Agreement as **Eclipse Day** from that year. The Agreement was signed by the then Maharaja of Manipur, Budhachandra Singh and Mr.V.P. Menon, Advisor to Government of India, and Shri Prakash, Governor of Assam on 21 September 1949. It was enforced on 15 October 1949. But the students were mainly concerned with the non-implementation of the Agreement in its letter and spirit. Article VIII of the Agreement reads as:

(1) The Government of India hereby guarantees either the continuance in service of the permanent members of the Public Services of Manipur on conditions which will be not less advantageous than those on which they were serving before the date on which the administration of Manipur is made over to the Government of India or the payment of reasonable compensation;

(2) The Government of India further guarantees the continuance of pensions and leave salaries sanctioned by

His Highness, the Maharaja to servants of the State who have retired or proceeded on leave preparatory to retirement ; before the date on which the administration of Manipur is made over to the Government of India.

(3) The Government of India also undertake to make suitable provisions for the employment of Manipuris in the various branches of Public Services; and in every way encourage Manipuris to join them. They also undertake to preserve various laws, customs and conventions prevailing in the state pertaining to social, economic and religious life of the people. These observances of Realization Day, Eclipse Day are but manifestations of the fear of **identity crisis** which operates in the collective mind of the student community.

On 29 July 1984 AMSU released a press-note criticising the indifferent attitude of the Government over the foreigners' issue in Jiribam. The Jiribam branch of AMSU had launched a class boycott strike from 27 June. The students were demanding detection and deportation of foreigners, inner-line permit system, inquiry into the missing of 1000 quintals of rice etc. On 11 July a joint meeting of the students and Government officials was held at the office of the SDO Jiribam. The officials persuaded the students to withdraw their two demands i.e. (1) introduction of inner-line permit and (2) inquiry into the missing rice. The students agreed to withdraw the two demands if the Government agreed to fulfil their other demands for not shifting 5th Manipur Rifles Battalion from Jiribam. On 29 July in a press-note, the Union asked whether the administration of Jiribam is handed over to the outsiders/foreigners.

On 9 October, the Union submitted a memorandum to the Union Home Minister through the Governor's Secretariat requesting him to solve the problem of Foreigners in the North East Region and inclusion of Manipuri in the VIII th Schedule of the Indian Constitution.

On the foreigners issue, AMSU passed several resolutions during the period 1982-90, but no overt action was seen at the political plane. AMSU organised, for instance, a North Eastern Students' Conference on 27-29 November, 1984. Kh. Loken Singh, President of AMSU forwarded the resolutions of the conference to the Prime Minister of India on 8 December, 1984. Some of the resolutions were, *4. Resolved that the Union and the Governments of states and union territories be given proper pressure to detect and deport foreign infiltrators, accordingly. Dispersal of the foreign infiltrators be made throughout the country, where deportation is not possible. Special provision be made so as to check the infiltrators from coming back armed with citizenship certificates from other states.*

5. Resolved that the Union Government be urged to introduce the Inner Line permit system, throughout the North East Region (where the system is not already introduced) as preliminary measure to check further infiltration of foreigners and that the execution thereof be left with the respective State or Union Territory Governments. It is further resolved to urge the Union Government to allow the state or union territory governments to issue permission to foreign tourists to visit the North East Region for a period not exceeding 15 days.

On 25 August 1985 a meeting of the Union was held the premises of Ghanapriya Women's College, Imphal. Many political personalities belonging to different political organizations and former Presidents of AMSU attended the meeting. The meeting discussed the steps taken by the

State Government to detect and deport foreigners so far in Jiribam area, mobilization of strength from the public etc. The meeting adopted the following resolutions:

1. That to urge the Government to implement the agreement reached between the Government to implement the agreement reached between the Government and AMSU over the issue of foreigners in 1980.
2. That to take up a new step with the help of public, if the Government failed to deport the foreigners/outsiders Student Volunteers Force organised an orientation course from 20 September at D.M.College of Science. During the course it delivered lectures on the following acts and rules;
    a. Foreigners Act of 1946
    b. Registration of foreigners Act 1939
    c. Indian Citizenship Act 1955
    d. Citizenship by Naturalisation of Territory
    e. Foreigners (Protected Area) order 1958.

It was to give knowledge of the Acts and Rules concerning foreigners so that they can mobilise other students within the purview of the detection and deportation of foreigners by constitution and law.

The same day, film slides entitled *Foreigners: a threat to our identity*, *Drive out foreigners* and *Include Manipuri in the VIII th Schedule* were screened at Asha Cinema Hall, North AOC point by the volunteers of AMSU.

Active actions, however, were mainly on opening schools affected by teacher-strikes (1982), Manipur University students strike demanding expulsion of Vice-Chancellor Ratho (1983); Neelam rape and murder case (1986), moves against the price rise (1986) etc.

In this background, AMSU needed an alternative process for accumulation of interest. So, AMSU took up the language issue in the limelight of the student politics though it was a regular feature in the charter of demands of the past years.

R.K. Itocha, President, AMSU in 1986-87 began to mobilize the mass in order to accumulate the interest over the language issue; but his main thrust was given actively on the rising prise, issue of cash memo, checking rationing agents. The language interest, however, is not rooted in AMSU activities and it was mainly spearheaded in earlier days by the Manipuri Sahitya Parishad, a literary body.

New Education Policy: National Goal Vs State Reality

The process of interest accumulation over language was disturbed by the phenomenal strike on the implementation of New Educational Policy without proper infrastructure in the State. Though NEP of 1986 aimed at attaining a good academic objective, AMSU argued that the ground reality in the state was not good environment of the policy; so they said *first infrastructure should be developed* prior to the implementation of the policy in Manipur. In order to implement the policy, the Government of Manipur had up-graded 21 high schools to higher secondary schools; and 13 colleges including leading colleges of D.M. College of Science, Imphal College were delinked from pre-university courses. It was the first step to abolish the pre-university course and to be replaced the same by XII class course under the NEP 1986.

In the developing situation, AMSU in its executive meeting on 9 August 1987 discussed the feasibility of the NEP 86 in the state. After a brief discussion, it was resolved that NEP 86 should not be implemented unless sufficient laboratory facilities, qualified teachers and other infrastructures were provided to the higher secondary schools and colleges. In order to draw attention of the authority, AMSU decided to boycott the forthcoming T.D.C. Examination, scheduled on 18 August and for effective action, an Action Committee of 40 students were formed. The Examination was disturbed and 59 students were arrested by police.

Irom Gambhir, President of AMSU sent a memorandum to the Union Minister of Human Resource and Development, suggesting five points as to the implementation of NEP 86 in the state;

(a) to allow and continue admission to P.U.C. classes in 13 colleges in which to P.U.C. classes have already been delinked with effect from the session 1987-88.

(b) to make available the required infrastructures such as providing adequate library, setting up of laboratory, extension of class rooms to the recently upgraded higher secondary schools;

(c) to allow Xi and XII classes in the upgraded higher secondary schools only after required infrastructures mentioned in (b) are fully met with;

(d) to appoint teachers through a proper appointing authority (i.e.) Manipur Public Service Commission) and to utilize the service of teachers so appointed at least one complete year in colleges in which P.U.C. classes are conducted. This arrangement will give some teaching experiences to the freshly appointed teachers to teach higher secondary courses;

(e) to revise the list of upgraded higher secondary schools by considering the following criteria:-

i. by considering the feeding school

ii. by considering the performance of schools.

iii. by considering scope for future expansion.

iv. by considering the population and geographical condition as well as communication infrastructures.

In persuasion of their demands, AMSU organised a procession of about 3000 students (reported) on 3 September, class boycott (11 September - 1 November), Rally of about 500 students at Oinam (16 September), street corner meetings for mass mobilization, Manipur Bandh (8-9 October), Public curfew of Government offices (19 October). Volunteers also set on fire one Maruti Gypsy (MNG 1716) of Adult Education at Wangkhei **Pujah** Lampak, On 7 October 1987 and a car (MNG 698) of Manipur Cycle Industries Co operation at Takyel on 8th October. On 9 October two jeeps MNG 390 of IFCD and MNG 680 of P.W.D. were simultaneously set on fire at Lamlong Bazar and Thangmeiband Watham Leirak.

On 17 October 1987 the Chief Minister called a press conference in his office chamber. It was attended by representatives of local and national newspapers and AIR etc. The C.M. clarified the stand of the Government and steps taken as follows:

1. R/R for appointment of teachers to Hr. Secondary have been amended. New R/R has been prepared and requisitions sent to MPSC and it has already issued notification and the advertisement is expected in the newspapers.
2. Regarding teachers' appointments without consulting the MPSC it was clarified that these appointments were of temporary nature and made in the interest of students of Hr. Sec. It was also clarified that their cases will be treated like fresh cases and MPSC will come to a decision on the basis of R.R. and eligibility and suitability.
3. As regards infrastructure in the upgraded schools like library books, science equipment and gas plant, it was clarified that the Government have already invited sealed tenders/quotations and supply order placed with firms. The items are expected very soon.
4. As regards the charge of AMSU that all the candidates who had passed Matric in 1987 have not been accommodated, the following statistic was placed, 10,012 candidates had passed in 1987. The total admission in the Hr. Sec. (including the newly upgraded) and colleges is 10,520.
5. Government also clarified that after a review it had undertaken of 21 upgraded schools, 2 out of the 21 upgraded schools, 2 out of the newly upgraded schools have been down graded, by an order dated 16.10.87. Regarding negotiation with the AMSU, it was clarified that doors were always open for negotiation and it was the AMSU which was not responding to the gestures of the

Government. All 62 arrested have been released unconditionally on 15-10-1987.

On 18 October a public meeting was convened by the guardians of Nambol protesting against the agitation of AMSU. It was attended by Th. Chaoba Singh, FCS Minister and H. Lokhon Singh. The speakers told the gathering that action against those students who disturbed the classes in the schools/colleges or damaged Government property would be taken.

On the same day, a press release was issued by All Manipur Youth Club, Yonglan Leirak. It appealed to the AMSU for a negotiation or talks with the Government within 21 October 1987. It further threatened AMSU that if the Union failed to do so, the club will take up further course of action w.e.f. 22 October. It says that the responsibility would be of the AMSU.

AMSU entered into negotiations with the Government of Manipur on 1 November 1987. The agreement, which was ultimately signed by Irom Gambhir, President of AMSU and K. Kipgen, Commissioner (Education) in the Government of Manipur reads as ;

1. The AMSU agrees in principle to the recent upgrading of High Schools to Higher Secondary School by the Government.
2. The Government of Manipur agrees in principle to the restoration of Pre-University First Year classes in any number of recently delinked colleges if the strength of student seeking admission warrants. This shall be implemented within 15 days from the date of agreement.
3. The Government of Manipur agrees that the

services of recently appointed 364 lectures in colleges and higher Secondary schools shall not be extended after the expiry of their six months' temporary appointments.

4. The Government of Manipur agrees that only those candidates recommended by the MPSC (except those otherwise disqualified) will be appointed on regular basis as lecturers in colleges and higher secondary schools.
5. The Government of Manipur agrees that the reservation of posts for SC/ST candidates shall be on subject-wise basis and it shall not exceed the percentage of quotas prescribed by the Reservation (Government of India) Rules, 1985.
6. The Government of Manipur agrees that seats reserved for SC/ST shall be treated as unreserved if suitable SC/ST candidates are not available as per rules.
7. The Government of Manipur agrees to withdraw all warrants cases, if any, against students for their involvement in the current AMSU Agitation and release immediately from jail all students arrested in this connection and that there shall be no victimization on this account.
8 The AMSU agrees to suspend their ongoing agitation with immediate affect.

But a fresh agitation started after a meeting of AMSU activists at D.M. College of Arts and Commerce, Imphal on 23 Nov. The meeting condemned the Government for non-implementation of the 1st November Agreement. There was a public debate in the newspapers in Imphal over the clause (2) where the words *if the strength of students seeking admission warrants.* Even the National Students' Union of India (NSUI), Manipur, in its leaflet, condemned the post-agreement activities of AMSU and asked *From the Government side, the Agreement was printed and circulated. Pressing to implement the matters* (in agreement) *is good for all of us. But, now the arguement* (put up by AMSU) *is what we meant was not this. What we would like to ask is, while you were signing the agreement what did you think of ?* AMSU tried to explain the circumstances and realities prevailing in the scene, but the Government remained silent.

So, AMSU once again started to boycott classes (2-5 Dec.) called a 46 hour Manipur Bandh (13 December), Mass agitation (22 December to 5 January 1988). And Ng. Devendra, General Secretary sent a memorandum on 29 Dec. 1987 expressing its stand after the agreement was signed on 1 November. It was said *After the agreement, the Director of Education (University) issued an* ***Admission Notice*** *inviting applications from the students who have not so far been admitted in any of the Higher Secondary Schools and colleges where P.U.C. had not been delinked. We confronted some of the officials to lift the restrictions and open admission to the students, who were rather forced to admit themselves in the newly upgraded schools including those students who had unwillingly admitted in the unauthorised private colleges. We argued that the denial of admission on non-availability of admission elsewhere should not be made pre-condition for opening P.U.C. classes in the delinked colleges. Later, the Government tried to justify the points of agreement and betrayed the spirit behind it.*

Meanwhile another batch of 51 (fifty one) temporary lecturers for the Higher Secondary and colleges were appointed on 30-11-87. It may be mentioned here that the

MPSC had already issued advertisement for the 355 post of lecturers and more then 2000 applications received. AMSU took this as irregular recruitment and an insult to the student community and general public. They expressed that all this was to justify their shady deals in the name of emergency, like contract works to **resourceful** contractors without open tender, supply orders to **approved** firms without open quotations and backdoor appointment of temporary lecturers to the Centre.

At the end, the issue could not be pulled on with the lack of lobbyists in the bureaucratic system and **confusion** over the *if* clause in the agreement even after the boycott of Republic Day 1988. The decision of the boycott was taken on 9 January 1988 in a meeting held at D.M. College of Arts and Commerce.

The positive side of the agitation was the re-construction of the AMSU and its relation to the public which were in an anticlimax state after the unresolved foreigners' issue.

LANGUAGE ISSUE

While the momentum of agitation was still warm, the newly elected President of AMSU, Mr. Y. Priyokumar was confronted with the GP. Women's College strike. The girl students were protesting the location of government quarters in the plot just adjacent to the college campus. It was on 11 September 1988, that a meeting of 55 students (including 15 girls) was held at D.M.College of Science, Imphal with the AMSU President in the chair. The meeting resolved to physically support the strike launched by the G.P. Women's College Students' Union. On 4 October, AMSU staged a procession to demand:

(a) A solution to Join Action Committee strike

(b) College Teachers' strike

(c) G.P.Women's College Strike and

Beside these, two other demands (i) Price control and (ii) Inclusion of Manipuri language in the Schedule VIII of the Indian Constitution were added.

As such, the accumulation of interest over the language issue was there. But a concerted effort or overt action in this regard was lacking. In a joint meeting held at D.M.College of Science on 15 March 1989, the language demand took centre-stage and the meeting took a resolution to mobilize the mass to this effect. The President of AMSU, later, sent two letters to the Prime Minister of India, one on 6 May to demand **job** facilities under Article VIII of Merger Agreement and another on 15 May to demand the inclusion of the language in the Schedule VIII. Earlier a letter was also sent in connection with the language demand on 11 January 1989 by him. In the letter, he noted that **Manipuri language may be compared with other scheduled languages of India** as follows:-

1. Mother tongue of the majority population in the concerned state;
2. Official language of the concerned state;
3. Language of the courts other than the High Court;
4. Primary medium of broadcast of All India Radio Programme;
5. Vehicle of an advanced and developed literature;
6. Medium of instruction and examination from primary to post graduate level.

In the next year (1989-90), the language demand was primarily focused along with other equally weighted demands of (a) Removal of Armed Forces (Assam and Manipur) Special Powers Act, 1958 and (b) Extension of Manipur Land Revenue and Land Reforms Act 1960 to the hill areas of Manipur. The first decision of the new President L. Gojendra and his executive council was for a concerted movement on the language demand and removal of the Act of 1958 from the state. On 27 August, the Hunger Marchers' Day, a public meeting was held at the historic Imphal Pologround, after a procession from Pishum Chingamacha to Imphal (about 5 kms). The meeting resolved to take action on (1) inclusion of Manipuri language in Schedule VIII (2) deletion of the word **Manipuri** as prefix or prefix to Bishnupriya (a small ethnic group in Assam who had been claiming as the original Manipuri although The group speaks a dialect of Indo-Iranian language), (3) enforcement of the Agreement on Foreigners' issue on 27 July and 5 August, 1980; (4) extension of the Manipur Land Revenue and Land Reforms Act, 1960 to the hill areas ;(5) enforcement of the agreement on the prohibition on selling and buying of immovable property in Imphal, Thoubal and Bishenpur districts of Manipur to outsiders by adding a sub section to sec. 158 of the Act of 1960 (the agreement was part of the Agreement on Foreigners Issue on 22 July and 5 August 1980) from the state. But, in subsequent action only the language demand, Act of 1958 and act of 1960 were given the main focus.

On 12 September, L. Gojendro and other student representatives submitted a memorandum to the Chief Minister demanding extension of Manipur Land Revenue and Land Reforms Act 1960 after a procession in Imphal. Their argument wasmainly based on the fact (a) that the law has its effect on only one-ninth of the state area, (b) that 90 percent of the food production is from this very small valley, (c) that there is no restriction in selling land in the valley area to any citizen of India resulting in increase of the density of population in Manipur valley day by day and widespread conversion of the cultivable lands/ fields into residential areas. A second procession of about 1000 students was staged in and around the market place of Imphal on 14 September. To press the demand, once more AMSU sent a letter to the Prime Minister of India on 28 October.

Meanwhile, the language demand became a political issue with more and more participating units. From 12 December, AMSU started a campaign for popularising the archaic Meitei script. It asked shops and establishments to use the Meitei archaic characters on posters and signboards in Imphal; it later spread to other areas of the state, especially the valley. For the first time in Manipur, the use of Meitei script in election posters wa seen in the Parliamentary and Assembly Elections of 1989 and1990. AMSU also started a signature campaign among the candidates of the Assembly Election on an undertaking of resignation if Manipuri language could not be included in the Schedule VIII of the Constitution and if the land law is not extended to the hill areas of the state. This signature campaign was launched from 8 February to 11 February 1990. Not a single Congress (I) candidate put his or her signature to the undertaking as it was not approved by the party high command.

That year, the Republic Day celebration was boycotted on various issues. The demands of language, Armed Forces Special Powers Act and the land law were raised alongwith two others which asked the government to save academic activities disturbed by the teachers' strike and that the administration should not be handed over to the outsiders. A leaflet emphatically asked citizens, *Let us be the master, not be servants*. But, they had already started violent actions from 23 January damaging many public properties in pursuit of their demands.

POLITICS OF THE SCRIPTS

The Meitei people is the only Tibeto-Burman speaker who has its own writing system and script. Different scholars have given different views on this. *Mr. Grierson, Dr. R. Brown and Dr. Suniti Kumar Chatterjee say that the Meitei script is a modification of the Indian scripts. Mr Damat says that the Meitei script was borrowed from Bengali during the reign of Charairongba at about 1700 A.D. and Mr. Hudson says that the Meitei script was borrowed from the Chinese at about 1540 A.D. which seem to have no foundation at all. Dr. Kalidas Nag says that the Meitei script is a pre-Ashokan script. Here Dr. Nag feels it is as old as 600 B.C.*[1] Ch. Manihar Singh[2] says, these views they cannot stand critical examination and are, therefore, not seriously taken in any quarter. Till now, the only available ground for ascertaining the time of its evolution is during the reign of Kiyamba (1467-1508) who first initiated the compilation of the royal chronicles otherwise known as the **Cheitharol Kumbaba** and a stone edict found at Khoibu village in the south east of Manipur. But another widely talked about period of emergence of the script is either at the end of 11th century or the beginning of 12th century when King Loyumba (1074-1112) issued a body of administrative rules and social codes known as the **Loyumba Sinyen**.

When Hinduism became the state religion in 18th century,

many cultural changes took place including the adoption of the Bengali script. Henry Damat said in 1877 that *The character has now been almost entirely superseded by Bengali, and indeed but few of the Manipuris can read it. A national chronicle is, however, still kept in the old character by the guild of priests* ***maibas*** *as they we called, in which every events of importance occurring in the country is regularly recorded*[3]. This view is contradicted by W. Ibohal in his statement that, *in the later part of the 19th century, modern Assamese and Bengali scripts began to replace the Meitei script slowly owing to the influence of British relations and absence of foundry and printing press in Meitei scripts. All common people began to learn the Bengali while the Meitei scripts were studied by royal Pandits and those who were interested in that field* [4].

The revivalists took the use of the Bengali script as a distortion of **national identity.** So, to them the re-introduction of the old Meitei script is part and parcel of the revival of pre-Hindu cultural heritage, which had been dominated by the Hindu ideology in general and Vaisnavism in particular. So, obviously some revivalists wanted the original 18 alphabet system (one of the four schools of script claimed to be the Meitei scripts). The political motive of the **Meetei Marup** founded by Naoriya Phulo of Cachar District of Assam is also obvious when it invented certain new characters and claimed to be the original old script. Later, the character were discarded by the local scholars and script experts. Some revivalists however like to adopt a 36 alphabet-system in order to enable the writers to spell the loan-words too.

On the other hand, Manipur Sahitya Parishad, a literary group formed by the Manipuri elite feels that the re-introduction of the Meitei script is a sign of continuity in the cultural change. In its fifth annual meeting, the Parishad took a resolution on the re-use of the Meitei script on 11 February 1940 which read as *Meitei script is our wealth; its loss is unfortunate; we must revive it. So, it is resolved to make efforts to this effect* (free translation of the resolution)[5]. Since then, the Parishad adopted the 36 character system of the Meitei writing.

Another radical view on the politics of the script is advocated by some youths having deviant political interest. They attacked the decision makers for every fate of the Meitei script. They explained the fate in terms of cultural hegemony of core Indians. They always try to explain all the socio-cultural conditions of the state in the light of **internal colonialism**. This political outlook became internalized in the youth and student socialization. To them, revivalism or continuity in change is meaningless unless there is a free political will of the society.

The Government of Manipur set up a Meitei Mayek Advisory Committee to examine the nature of the Meitei script. As the Committee could not bring out any visible result another body, Meitei Mayek Experts Committee was formed in 1979 under the patronage of the Government. It *was constituted in accordance with the explicit instructions of the Manipur Legislative Assembly to decide which of the four schools of indigenous script is to be adopted by the Government*[6]. After 24 sittings spread over a period of eight months, the Expert Committee unanimously recommended a system of 27 indigenous letters to be recognised and adopted as the Meitei script. All the letters which do not represent the present Manipuri pronunciation was taken out from the 36 character system. But, in spite of the various Government promises, the script could not be reintroduced till now. Any political action with an interest in script could not be carried out independently. AMSU took up the script as a means to mobilize the mass for their language movement in L. Gojendra's time.

In the meantime, the months from February to June, AMSU boycotted classes to condemn the alleged assault of K. Chingkham, Secretary General of AMSU by Home Minister I. Tompok in later's office chamber. It staged rallies (10 March at Moirang, 21 March at Thoubal, 26 March at Kakching), **Bandh** (11 June at Imphal market area, 14 June in greater Imphal, 16 June vehicle Bandh at state level); disturbed the functioning of Government offices (25-30 June). The loss of public property during the height of AMSU activities are given below:

Date	*Place of occurrence*	*Nature of the damage*
23 January	Imphal	1. Set fire southern wing of the Shyamasakhi Girl's High School, and Bengali High School.
24 January	Khuman	Set fire 3 Maruti gypsies, all belonging to Directorate of Social Welfare and Art and Culture MNG 2665, 2667, 2668)
24 January	Keishamthong	Set fire a car MNG 851 Imphal
24 January	Minuthong	Set fire a Tata truck (MNG 746) belonging to I.F.C.D.
25 January	Meino Leirak	Set fire a tata truck (MNS 9925) 26 January Imphal Pelting stone at different places. Damage by pelting of a scooter (MNB 6078).

Unparalleled in Gojendra's period was the protest against the attempted molestation of a girl student by Dr. Harlal

Saha, a senior lecturer of Chemistry in D.M. College of Science, who came to him for private tuition; and M. Deven Singh, Minister of State for assaulting 3 students on 16 April 1990. Saha's case ended with the termination of his service after a disciplinary proceeding. The Governor's order No.4/261/89-S/SE dated 20 June reads as:

Whereas disciplinary proceedings were initiated against Dr. Harlal Saha, Lecturer (selection grade), D.M. College of Science, Imphal on charges relating to giving private tuition on receiving payment from students and misbehaviour with a female student;

Whereas the Inquiry Officer found the above charges to have been established against the said Dr. Harlal Saha.

And whereas an inquiry was conducted in the said charges by the Commissioner, Departmental Inquiries, Manipur;

And whereas the Inquiry Officer found the above charges to have been established against the said Dr. Harlal Saha and that the Governor of Manipur is satisfied with the findings;

And whereas the Governor of Manipur, having regard to the findings of Inquiry Officer decided to impose provisionally, as the findings on two charges warranted imposition of major penalty jointly or severally, the penalty of compulsory retirement under Rule-II (VII) of the Central Civil Services (classification, control & appeal) Rule after consulting the Manipur Public Service Commission have no consideration of the Inquiry Report agreed with the proposal for imposition of the above major penalty vide their letter No.5/11/90-DE/MPSC dated 19th June, 1990.

Now, therefore, the Governor of Manipur is pleased to order imposition of the major penalty of Compulsory Retirement on Dr. Harlal Saha, Lecturer (S.G.), D.M. College of Science, Imphal under Rule II (VI) of the Central Civil Service (Classification, control & Appeal) Rules 1965 with immediate effect. The order was signed by Naved Masood, the secretary to the Government of Manipur. The girl student was given a reward of Rs.500/- for her moral courage vide Memo No.1/8/5-SE-78 dated 6 May 1990.

In the **Deven case,** AMSU asked the Chief Minister to drop M. Deven from the ministry for his act of assault on 3 student leaders on the night of 16 April. The student leaders were reportedly on a errand for observance of **Realization Day** being organised on 17 April to pay homage to the victims of 1980 police firing on the agitating students.

Later, on 6 May 1990, in a discussion between the representatives of AMSU led by L. Gojendra, President, AMSU and the Chief Minister brought a solution. In a letter to L. Gojendra Singh from Mr. S. Ibohal Singh, Minister of State dated 6 May 1990 says that *I am to convey the decision that Shri M. Deven Singh would remain as Honourable Minister of State without portfolio upto the end of October, 1990. Further I am happy for the assurance committed by the AMSU representatives not to press further on the issue of Shri Deven Singh, Honourable Minister of State without portfolio if he does not repeat the misbehaviour in future and also to withdraw their protest agitation.*

Bishnupriya Problem and AMSU

The Bishnupriya issue was not a problem directly affecting the state of Manipur. Time and again, the problem was discussed in various political platforms as a reaction to the Bishnupriya move to usurp the rights of Manipuris residing in the state of Assam. The cultural organizations, student bodies and political parties in Manipur were responding to the call of cultural organizations in Assam representing the Manipuris.

The Manipuris in Assam say, the Bishnupriya is the descendent of Dooms and other Bengalis of low caste. Their occupation was originally that of the supplying grass for royal stables. They speak a language which is different from that of the true Manipuris and is in fact closely allied to vulgar Bengali. It belongs to the Eastern Bengal, mainly concentrated in the Sylhet areas. According to the 1971 census, there are about 43813 in India (only about 33591 lived in Assam and about 9884 in Tripura). The Bishnupriya in Manipur are well assimilated in the larger Manipuri social system.

Even the Government of Manipur, time and again, showed sign of protest to such a claim that the Bishnupriya is Manipuri or part of it. The latest Memorandum on Bishnupriya submitted to the Prime Minister of India was that of Mr. R.K. Ranbir, on 5 October, 1980. Among others, it was said that *In the meantime, the Bishnupriya community have been agitating for adding the prefix* ***Manipuri*** *to their community and language to the extent of distorting the history of Manipur in a recent Memorandum submitted to you and the Union Home Minister followed by some statements of their leaders at New Delhi. They made fantastic claims of being the original Manipuris, speaking an Aryan language having links with Arjuna-Chitrangada, and also claimed that they had been suppressed by people of Tibeto-Burman origin (i.e. the present Manipuris). Now they demand that their language should also be included along with Manipuri, in the 8th Schedule to the Constitution of India. Needless to say that when the news was flashed in some national dailies,* *it provoked strong reactions among the Manipuris of Manipur, Assam and Tripura. This anti-national act has even threatened to uproot the spirit of social harmony in the sensitive north-eastern region.*

> *...the present Bishnupriya community was originally called* ***Kalisha*** *(children of Mother Kali) or* ***Kalichhaya*** *(owing to their dark complexion) by the Manipuris. Following a mass exodus, this group who stayed in Rangamati (of Chittagong Hill District) migrated later to Udaipur in South Tripura and came to Manipur during the reign of King Khagemba (1697-1652). They were allowed to settle at the village Lamangtong and the neighbouring areas. King Jai Singh (1759-1798) shifted his capital from Imphal to Lamangtong and called it Bishnupur (1776), and hence they were referred to as* ***Bishnupriyas*** *by the historians when the Burmese forces defeated the King of Manipur and occupied the land (Known as Seven Years' Devastation in the history of Manipur) a mass exodus took place (1819-1826) and many Manipuris and Bishnupriyas left for Assam, Tripura and Bangladesh (former Sylhet Region of East Bengal). King Gambhir Sing (18125-1834) had then converted them into the Vaishnavite religion.*

Through the historical process of assimilation they became integrated with the language and culture of the Manipuris. They became Manipuris and hence there is not a single Bishnupriya family in Manipur. This statement is based on the latest findings in research on the part of the scholars of Manipur.

> *....in the light of the above observations, the Manipuris can never be divided into two communities viz. Manipuri Meitei and Manipuri Bishnupriyas. Linguistically and ethnically the Kalishas / Bishnupriyas have a separate identity and should not be mixed up with the Manipuris or Meiteis.*

The fact that the Bishnupriyas who speak an Indo-Aryan dailect should not be grouped with Manipuri/Meitei, a Tibeto-Burman language and that the Bishnupriyas cannot claim to be Manipuris has been confirmed also by (a) the Census Centenary Monograph No.10(1971) (b) the letter of the Assistant Commissioner, Linguistic Minority in India, (of 6-12-1977) addressed to three Bishnupriya Associations... and (c) the letter of the Assistant Commissioner for Linguistic Minorities in India (of 16-11-1988) addressed to the President, Nikhil Bishnupriya Manipuri Sahitya Parishad, Silchar.

The President of AMSU, L. Gojendra continued to take a special interest in the issue. He sent a memorandum to the Chief Minister of Assam on the 15 October 1989 saying that the order of the Government of Assam, dated July 21, 1989 has defiled and amputated the Manipuri language by confusing the same with a dialect, purportedly called **Bishnupriya.** It is against the spirit of Article 29 (1) of the Constitution of India which conserves the Manipuri language. The unconstitutional order has also disgraced the Manipuri speaking people all over the country.

> ...the Hiteswar Saikia ministry took not more than 24 days to stay its unconstitutional order dated 14 November 1983 which disgraced the Manipuri language; but unfortunately, the present Assam Ministry has failed to revoke or nullify its constitutional order, dated July 21st, 1989 even after 85 days of committing this grave injustice...
>
> *The All Manipur Students' Union, Manipur hereby beseech your good self and the Ministry of Assam not only to kindly revoke the order dated 14.11.83 passed by the Hiteswar Saikia Ministry forthwith without any further delay once for all in the larger interest of the Manipuri*

> *society so as to enable us to maintain the everstanding social and cultural integrity between the Manipuris and Assamese.*

Besides the language inclusion in the list of Schedule VIII, L. Gojendra mentioned in his memorandum to the Prime Minister of India, a point on Bishnupriya which said- *The recognition of* ***Bishnupriya Manipuri*** *language as the medium of instruction at primary school level in Assam has been stayed with effect from 17th Oct. 1989 until further orders by the Government of Assam. In the meantime, the Govt. of Assam will be the obtaining clarification from the Government of India* (Commissioner of Linguistic Minorities), *in this regard. In this context, the All Manipur Students' Union hopes that the Honourable Prime Minister shall give due attention so as to prevent Manipuri being added as either suffix or prefix to Bishnupriya language.*

The Government of Assam responded positively with a Press Note (No.99 of 17 October 89) which read - *The Government of Assam has received representations from various organizations and associations submitting objections to the decision for instructions at the primary level. The objections have been mainly for the use of the word* ***Manipuri*** *along with* ***Bishnupriya*** *In the view of this it has been decided to keep the decision... in abeyance until further orders. In the meanwhile, clarification will be obtained from the Government of India (Commissioner of Linguistic Minorities) in this regard.*

The Manipuri-Bishnupriya tension or rather conflict over the ethnonyme, which started in the first quarter of the century, played a good role in solidifying these minority groups in Assam. This activated in both the communities a collective need for preservation of their own identities.

But, the conflict was not able to create a catalyst for solidarity formation in Manipur. It is however true, that the Manipuris in Manipur took interest in this conflict only because of the Pan Manipuri collectivity. AMSU, this time, took up the issue of Bishnupriya because the issue might pose a serious threat to the movement of the inclusion of the Manipuri language in the Schedule VIII to the Constitution. During the language movement, the students felt that *language is the alternative name of the Manipuri culture and identity and hence, there is no culture if there is no recognition of the language.*

R.K. Bobichand: Another Constitutional Crisis in AMSU

R.K. Bobichand, General Secretary of the Imphal College Students' Union, took over as AMSU President on 30 July 1990. The first month of his term was devoted to the organization of the AMSU Silver Jubilee Celebrations of AMSU Silver Jubilee which continued for 4 days. For the mega event, AMSU needed a huge amount of money. It had collected a sum of Rupees 1,03, 580/- (One lakh, three thousand five hundred and eighty) from different shops/ hotels and other sources in Imphal town. With grand success AMSU celebrated its colourful Silver Jubilee (27-30 August) with various programmes and humble homage to those souls who lost their lives in police firing on 27 August 1965.

Immediately after the 4-day celebration, AMSU was confronted with the **rape and murder of a student.** R.K. Tamphasana was reportedly gangraped and murdered. She was a student of P.U. (Commerce) in Modern College of Imphal. As she passed the final examination in 1990, she had gone to the college on 27 August to collect her mark sheet. But, her dead body was found on 29 August in the

Imphal river, near Mahabali Hanuman temple complex, Imphal. The post mortem report reflected that she had been gangraped and murdered. (Her case was the second of its kind in Imphal. The first one occurred in 1986 ; the victim was one Neelam Panchabhaiya. A Students' Action Committee was formed with Mr. R.K. Itocha, President of Manipur University Students' Council as the Chairman. The Committee submitted a memorandum to the Governor's Secretary and the Chief Minister on 19 April 1986 to hand over the case to C.B.I. or to institute a judicial enquiry. The case had not been completed for want of evidence including the post mortem report). For the Tamphasana Case, AMSU submitted a memorandum to the Chief Minister on 5 September to investigate the case properly and punish the criminals. Many other organisations including the informal associations of **Meira Paibi** (informal and voluntary association of the Meitei women) were also pressing the Government of Manipur to this effect.

In the month of September, there were a series of violent actions. The demands varied from non-availability of textbooks to the **Tamphasana case.** These actions were claimed as being done by the AMSU. Some of the actions were (a) blasting of one big-size firecracker in the campus of Director of Education (S) office (13 September); (b) blasting of firecracker in the office campus of Director of Education (U) (13 September); (c) blasting of two firecrackers at B.T. Road (13 September); (d) attempt to set fire the office building of Central Census (19 September).

Mr. Bobichand called on the Chief Minister on 20 September in connection with the Tamphasana case. The President, AMSU was accompanied by 11 other representatives (including Finance Secretary, Joint

Secretary, Vice President, General Secretary and three members of Students' Voluntary Committee of AMSU). The Chief Minister assured them that the **real culprits** of the case will be arrested. But, the Singjamei Unit of AMSU was reluctant to accept the Chief Minister's assurance. At the second round of negotiations, President R.K. Bobichand, Secretary General Brojen Loitongbam and a SVC member sat with Chief Minister on 25 September. The negotiation with the AMSU representatives could not help or bring out any clues to the investigation of the case because of the fact that the real criminals could not be identified then. There were rumours of involvement of sons/men of some VIPs, but no hard evidence was found.

By October, AMSU faced an internal conflict between the President and Finance Secretary. On 13 October, the President of AMSU suspended six members of Executive Council, leaving aside the Vice President and the General Secretary. The six-men-group claimed, on 14 October, that they had 2/3 majority of the Executive Council of AMSU in their favour. They selected an acting General Secretary (L.C. Meenabanta) and formed a 4-member Presidential Committee. The founder members, founder office bearers and ex-office bearers tried to make a compromise of the two groups in a joint meeting on 27 November and 2 December. The decision could not bind either of the parties. The Khurai Unit of AMSU expressing pain in the crisis in the Executive Council took three resolutions on the the problem. It boldly said that the Unit would not co-operate either of the parties unless they work unitedly. The decision was taken on 11.11.1990. Once more the efforts of founder members, founder office bearers and ex-office bearers, besides the student community, could not put the AMSU together again.

The AMSU of 1990 was no more a simple and less differentiated body as that of 1965. It had became a complicated and complex body and hence, its internal problems sometimes could not be solved on the basis of appeals of groups and the general public. The course of events took a sharp U-turn with the kidnapping of President R.K. Bobichand on 12 November. It was reported that he was kidnapped by some unidentified gunmen from a lane in Paona Bazar near the Laisana Press in the evening of 10 November. But, he was found later released at a place in between Ningthoukhong and Thinungei of Bishenpur District unconditionally on 13 November. The kidnappers could not be traced as he said that he was taken blindfold and kept in a room in the same fashion.

Prior to the kidnapping, in a meeting of 13 October 1990, AMSU (Bobichand) took other five resolutions, besides the suspension of 6 Secretaries ; they were (i) removal of cabins from the hotels (because in these cabins, many immoral activities were reportedly done); (ii) banning of obscene pictures in the cinema halls; (iii) finalization of **Tamphasana case**; (iv) observation of **Eclipse Day** on 15 October; (v) observation of Language Demand Day on 2nd November and to start street/public meeting. They organized a rally on 26 November and boycotted classes of all the educational institutions (29-30 October).

The line of action of AMSU (Bobichand) slightly changed in the month of November. It called an economic blockade (4-6 November). Two other demands were also added to previous list of demands, they were (a) inclusion of Manipuri language in Schedule VIII and (b) withdrawal of Armed Forces (Assam and Manipur) special Power act, 1958. During the blockade, two violent incidents were reported, attack with patrol bomb on Tata Truck (MN 01-3334) causing injury to the driver on 4 November ; and set fire on one Toyota truck of Imphal Municipality bearing registration plate No. M N 01-G 828 at Ucheckon on 5 November. The final talk with the Chief Minister was convened on 25 November.

The other group, commonly known as AMSU (Chingkham) because of the fact that he was one of the members of the Presidential Committee, also acted for the **Tamphasana Case.** They called for a Manipur Bandh (14-15 November). During the Bandh, a Maruti Gypsy of PHED was set fire on University Student Bus (MNG 11171) one jeep of Department of Electricity (MNG 523) and one jeep of UNICEP (MNG 1695) were also set fire on 14 November and another Jeep (MNG 523) of Electricity Deptt. was set fire at Moirangkhom Bazar, pelting of stone, dismantling of bridge were also reported from different parts of Imphal during the Bandh hours.

In spite of factionalism, the political actions of AMSU as such were appreciated by the general mass; the level of people's participation in general interests like language issue, demand for removal of Act of 1958 was high. The **Tamphasana Case** however, did not achieve a logical conclusion. It was the same in the **Neelam Panchavaya case** of 1986. The naked truth was that the political bosses always intervene leaving the state police utterly helpless in investigating such high profile cases. Bodies like AMSU could only shout and shout for justice to end up in frustation.

Another remarkable action of AMSU was against the inclusion of the **Meitei** in O.B.C. list under the Mandal Commission Report. MUSU organized a two-day symposium on the issue on 29-30 September, 1990. The panel discussion, participated by Dr. Ch. Manihar, Dr. Ch. Budhi, Dr. Ksh

Bimola, Dr. Ph. Sumitra, Y. Sadananda (President of MUSU) and R.K. Bobichand (President of AMSU) on 1 October *proposed to the Government of Manipur (a) to re-examine Mandal Commission's methodology and criteria as applied to the case of the Meiteis, taking into account the empirical picture of the social structure of the people, (b) to revise the list of other Backward Classes for Manipur given in Vol. VI of the report as the domiciled status of many of them is doubtful and (c) to study minutely how far practical gains can be had by the Meiteis after joining the OBC in terms of Public Services and other material benefits.*

REFERENCES

1. W Ibohal Singh, *History of Manipur,* Imphal, 1986:504-505
2. Ch Manipur Singh, *A Clarification on the Bishnupriyas in relation to the Manipuris,* Manipuri Sahitya Parishad, 1987:30
3. Guybor H Damat, "Note on the Old Manipuri Character" in *Journal of Asiatic Society of Bengal,* Vol. XLVI, pt.I, 1877:36
4. W Ibohal Singh, op.cit.:505
5. As quoted in *Sovenier,* Manipuri Sahitya Parishad, 1980:35
6. Th Tarunkumar (ed) *Resistance,* a weekly, Vol. IV No. 31, Pan Manipuri Youth League, Imphal, 7 August, 1979

7

AMSU IN MANIPUR POLITICAL SYSTEM

A participating unit in the political system AMSU acts as a pressure group having diffused authority and diffused interests. Even though it is not reflected in its constitution, the political interest of this student body is predominantly regional oriented. The primary concern of the body is, of course, Manipur-centric. But, AMSU takes the common issues of North-East India into consideration while it takes political decision or acts. As a matter of fact, AMSU has no link directly or indirectly with any of the regional political parties including the largest of such parties, Manipur People's Party because of its apolitical formation. The regional parties were popularly taken as **the tail of Congress** or **spring board of Manipur politicians** and power is often synonymous with the Congress. In the political culture of Manipur, there are two poles, pro-constitutionalist and anti-constitutionalist, which are popularly known as **power-politics** and **anti-government politics**. In the first pole, the Congress has no match; on the other hand, the anti-establishment ideology is mainly dominated by alienated youths of non-associational interest groups. MPP seldom creates public opinion on political issues, rather it tries to catch votes by supporting issues originating from the alienated youth pressure groups.

Regionalism as an ideology which operates in the system environment of student politics again consists of two poles. The Manipur People's Party and many other small parties in the state represent pro-constitutionalist regionalism. They dream of a brighter Manipur within the framework of Indian constitution. But all the unlawful political groups such as the United National Liberation Front representing Anti-India separatist regionalism dream of an Independent State. On the other hand, the pro-constitutionalist regionalism is being continually tested by its regional tendency to demand or project Manipuri identity, pride and respectable position in the entire **National system**. The political demands of statehood and language in the Indian constitution, employment facilities to Manipuris under Article VIII (3) of the Merger Agreement of 1949, reservation quota through inclusion of the Meetei in Other Backward Category list are some of the reflections of pro-constitutionalist regionalism. But, the other pole does not consider such demands as an important political demands. They like to examine the economic relation between Manipur and India, political freedom, the operation of **captive market** etc. at the foremost layer of the body politic of the state.

AMSU, in this environment, does not act explicitly in either of the poles. Though there were certain press releases which sound anti-constitution regionalism, their demands always fell under the pro-constitution category. However, the student body always maintains its neutralality to parties interests and ideology, AMSU, while acting as a pressure group, does not negate the constitutional spirit, but the propaganda overtones of the student group during agitation create a significant information flow to **deviant political actors**. This paradoxical position of AMSU, sometimes, mislead the observers towards anti-constitution regionalism.

At another level of political culture, the so-called 'revivalism' operates with a Meitei ethnocentric attitude. The body social of contemporary Manipuri society is dominated by the synthetic complex Hindu elements and the pre-Hindu Meitei elements. The revivalists like to discard Hindu elements which had the upper hand in the Meitei kingdom (especially during the reign of Maharaj Churachand(1891-1941). In spite of the revivalist religious fundamentalism, the movement effected some positive influence to the political system like in the demands of re-introduction of the ancient script after a period of about half a century, secularization of the educational institutions. The 'love of pre-Hindu Manipur' had dramatic political pragmatism because it meant the search of a political identity having Southeast roots as opposite to the Hindu thesis that the Manipuris are the descendents of Brabubahan, the son of Arjuna and hence of Aryan origin hypothesis of this ethnic group.

AMSU is not a revivalist group but the politics of the revivalist ideology has a great impact on the students' mind. The manifestation of the ideology is often noticed in many leaflets circulated during various agitations. But, the major difference between the AMSU and the revivalist groups is that the former is free from the fundamentalist ideology which is the core part of the latter. The secularization of educational institutions was an important issue in late 70's which was initiated and spearheaded by AMSU, but it did not amount to mere negation of the Hindu Saraswati **Puja**. No doubt, the issue provoked many individuals or groups in different ways thereby evoking different responses during the movement. But, AMSU was able to project a stance which is neutral and as a upholder of the constitutional principle of secularism; while the revivalists interpreted the success of the movement as a win over the Hindu elements.

In such an environment, AMSU was able to receive political information and take decisions independently. The highest authority of AMSU, no doubt, is the Executive council but due weightage is given to the general opinion expressed members of the Student Volunteer Committee (SVC). Though it is not mentioned in AMSU constitution, the role of SVC is permanent and hence, a non-partisan ideology could not be not maintained. While choosing demands in the interest of the **public**, the worldview of SVC and the personality of the President obviously play a part. Some demands are an end-in-itself while some others are a means for attaining certain other ends. Still there are demands which are meant for creating **public awareness** of the existing political objective conditions. These are designed with a major participation of the SVC. The one year tenure of executive body, theoretically, cannot articulate the long-term aspirations and momentum of certain issues.

Because of this special organizational setup of the AMSU, political demands vary with the change of guard. The demand of **foreigner deportation** in 1980 was changed dramatically to the **language issue** in late 1980's. In some cases, political demands are seen to be a projection of the moderate Meitei nationalism. The game over **secularism** in late 1970s was very tactfully played; the demands and agitation for it made the people aware of the political reality associated with the Meiteis religious outlook and of the changing political culture, as well. It was not altogether a moderate contra-acculturation move, but rather, the aspiration of a wider political goal associated with the general desire of youths for more freedom. Therefore, the demands generally raised reflect a predominant ideology which is more or less safeguarded by the SVC, beside other like-minded youth organizations. One may note that, any input to the larger political system is always in the form of demands, and not of support to a government decision. If they do not agree to a stance of the government, they agitate. Otherwise, they remain silent.

An anti-establishment attitude manifest in their general demand is always reflected in the techniques adopted by them in their agitation and/or movements. Public meeting and street corner meetings, propaganda leaflets expressing the merits of the demand and the government's step motherly treatment, boycott of national festivals and sabotage are the most common techniques on certain demands. Sometimes, student activists supporting AMSU even went to the extent of showing disrespect to national symbols or figures. This is however, not a peculiarity of AMSU. It has roots in general Manipuri ambivalence towards the Indian nationhood. The Manipuri youth has a sceptical mind of their meaning in the Indian mainstream. The expression of such a psychic state is painful, but the AMSU agitators can get youths' support with the denial of national elements. The techniques and their manifestation, however, in larger systemic terms, are interwined with the ever growing problem of insurgency - the conflict between the elite personality and the newly emerged youth personality, at the psychological level. Though insurgency is quite a different phenomenon, student politics in the state, time and now, is cybernetically related with the problem. The insurgent groups may not be able to command student politics in the state; but, the youths as ignified by the techniques of AMSU agitation may become more easily available potential to these insurgent groups. The situation is more aggravated by the existing political culture of the state.

Though the political culture of Manipur has two antagonistic poles of the pro-constitutionalist and the anti-constitutionalist, the social system is dominated by the passive deviant. These deviants feel, there are inconsistencies in the system prevailing in the state. Still, they were not ready to join the anti-constitutionalist pole either. They try to maintain their existing status-quo as well as to generate the **angry** youth's energy to challenge certain structural units in the system. This reality in the existing system help AMSU to command mass support in any agitation against the established order. It is notable here, too, that the age-old **out-group** attitude of the Manipuris to the **Mayangs** or outsiders mainly from core India, directly or indirectly, motivates the negation of national elements. The **Mayangs** play a vital role in the colonial Manipur economy and public administration. R. Constantine notes very clearly of the **Anti-Mayang** attitude: *The local people give Mayangs a wide berth, if they can help it. Seldom does a Manipuri go out of his way to make friends with the mayangs. You are rarely asked in unless you happen to be particularly close to someone in the house. Where you are no more than an acquaintance, a Manipuri is taciturn. A Mayang who is a hail-follow-well-met is struck by the humility with his hosts refer to him. He is honoured, greatly and sincerely so. But, by and large, Manipur seems to tell you,* ***Love me, but keep out. A certain exclusiveness born out of insular living is palpably there*[1].**

This attitude is transformed in many ways in general youth's perception of the government as the **Den of Mayang** and hence, any agitation against them is socially accepted. Rather it is well supported by the passive deviants. The young students, while showing their anger against price hike or Manipur's deteriorating economy, show the unconscious hatred rooted in their collective psyche. It is because of this faith, AMSU did not lose its mass base even at times of internal crisis or factionalism.

Moreover, people in the larger social system look forward to the demands of AMSU as antibiotic to Manipur's present day inability. They have no organized and alternative outlet to their ever increasing frustration mainly over economic shortcomings and political meaninglessness. The existing political parties are seen by the general people as formal groupings of individuals having a common vested interest in power. People also feel, these parties seldom think or speak of people's grievances, aspirations and desires. They juggle with popular issues only to **catch votes** at the time of elections. On the other hand, the apolitical student body is culturally imaged as the champion of public interests. But AMSU face a lot of trouble in dealing with the clash of interests generated by different social groups as it does not have a permanent and well-defined political ideology. Because of the diffused responsibility, AMSU cannot deny the opinion of a particular group and sometimes it cannot entertain two contrasting opinions at the same time.

Coming back to the relation of AMSU to its sociopolitical environment, the information flow of this student body is linked with many units and groups. Some information are taken for granted and AMSU readily starts action thereon. But, general information are sorted out by AMSU on the **regionality** mainly concerned with historical pride, survival of the Manipuris, regional economy, revivalism, demographic profile, territorial integrity. No doubt, at a particular point of time AMSU may sometimes harp upon Meitei chauvinism. Because of this sorting out mechanism, AMSU and the national political parties such as Indian National congress(I), Communist Party of India, Janata Dal, Communist Party of India (Marxist) or their political wings have limited information flow. This does not mean that AMSU does not take national parties into consideration while taking any decision; the relation between it and the regional parties is more sensitive than that with other parties.

Again, information flow is often disturbed by ethnic based demands or interests like the issues of Greater Nagaland or Southern Nagaland, Zeliangrong state demand or Kuki homeland. Although it stands for the wider student community comprising all the students in Manipur, AMSU seldom engages the other ethnic based student bodies on the above mentioned issues. Since inception, AMSU has stood for an integrated Manipur and it leaves no room for negotiations on the issue of **disintegration** of the present geographical area known as Manipur. Unlike many tribal bodies, AMSU strongly assert that **Manipur is more than a mere geographical entity.** Because of certain psycho-political reasons accumulated since the British days, the tribal students too had reservations in showing solidarity to AMSU, especially during the post-Foreigner agitation period. The sphere of influence of the Muslim student bodies is however limited both in student politics and the state system.

In the entire period under study (1965-1992), AMSU was able to put forward issues of importance and on many occasions it suceeded in effecting changes in government policies and stance. But, due to the inherent weakness of the short tenure of its Executive Council, the demands of the student body are often twisted by the Government. Many of the assurances, agreements on major issues vanishes in thin air even before implementation. This is mainly due to (1) red tapism in administrative machineries; (2) frequent change of ministry or government; or (3) defects in the terms and conditions of the agreements or the government's deliberate design of doing so with ambiguous terminology.

The AMSU activists can be very good agitators, they are not always good negotiators. Besides this, AMSU seldom succeed in manoeuvring the bureaucratic labyrinth. The process stop once the agreements are inked and it also could not conjure up a matching strategy for overcoming beaucratic hurdles.

But, the agreements which were not implemented, operate in its feedback loop to generate collective frustration in the youth psyche. The political actions of AMSU are not ends in itself. The positive outcome is directed toward an order of **democratic and rational** enculturation of the social actors in the state. The agitations bring to focus the aspirations of the people on a political plane. In the process, the articulation of rights and aspirations become widespread.

The negative outcome, however, makes a short cut to the deviant subculture in the state system. This is linked with the entire motivational orientation of the anti-constitutionalist pole. The delicate position of AMSU is, however, not fully felt by the government.

On the other way round, AMSU is blamed for unsuccessful agitations by the general public. As the STUDENT-PUBLIC relation is cathartic in nature universally, the failure of AMSU in negotiation causes a corresponding frustration in the public mind. The failure is often percieved by the general public not in terms of skill deficiency with regard to negotiations, but with a suspicious eye to the negotiators of the student body even to the extent of being bought by the government with money or facilities. The government can well play with this cathartic relation of AMSU and the public.

The last line may thus be written in summing up the evaluation of AMSU political action: AMSU still acts as **an impartial and neutral body with a wide range of interests.** But, it will wrong to say that AMSU is a good angry young man, and not a good young politician.

REFERENCE

1. R Constantine, *Manipur: Maid of Mountain,* New Delhi, 1981

BIBLIOGRAPHY

Primary Sources

AMSU Soveniers of different years

AMSU Guard Files

Police Records of student activities of different years

Journals

N K Sanajaoba, ed., *Lamyanba,* Pan Manipuri Youth League, Imphal

Th Tarunkumar, ed, *Resistance,* Pan Manipuri Youth League, Imphal

North East History Association Proceedings, Shillong

Local Dailies

Hueiyen Lanpao

Ihou

Khollao

Manipur Mail

Paojel

Prajatrantra

Simanta Partika

Books and Articles

A C Netrajit, *All Manipur Silver Jubilee 1965-1990 Souvenir,* AMSU, Imphal, 1990

Aikara, Jacob, *Ideological Orientation of Student Activism, Poona, 1977*

Almond, Gabriel A and G B Powell, Jr, *Comparative Politics,* Little Brown, London, 1978

Altbach, Philip G, *The Student Revolution: a Global Analysis,* Lalvani, Bombay, 1970

Barua, Indrani, *Pressure Groups in Assam,* Omsons, New Delhi, 1990

Cady, John F, *South East Asia: Its Historical Development,* Tata McGraw Hill, New Delhi, 1976

Ch Manihar Singh, *A Clarification on the Bishnupriyas in relation to the Manipuris,* Manipuri Sahitya Parishad, Imphal, 1987

China Quartery, relevant issues

Cockburn, Alexander and Robin Blackburn, *Student Power,* Penguin, London, 1969

Constantine, R, *Manipur: Maid of Mountain,* New Delhi, 1981

Dahl, Robert A, *Modern Political Analysis,* PHI, New Delhi, 1989

Damat, G H, "Note on the Old Manipuri Character" in *Journal of the Asiatic Society of Bengal,* Vol XLVI, pt.I, Calcutta, 1877

David Easton, *A System Analysis of Political Life,* John Wiley, New Delhi, 1965

Deka, Meeta, *Student Movement in Assam,* Vikas Publishing House, Delhi, 1996

Douglas, Stephen A and Bachtiar, Harsja, "Indonesian Students: Generation of 1966" in Philip G Altbach, *The Student Revolution: a Global Analysis,* Lalvani, Bombay, 1970

Easton, David, "An Approach to the Analysis of Political System" in Stephen V Monsma and Jack R V D Slik, *American Politics,* Holt, New York, 1970

Encyclopedia Americana

Fadia, Babulal, *Pressure Groups in Indian Politics,* Radiant, New Delhi, 1980

Grierson, *Linguistic Survey of India, Vol III pt. III*

Hall, D G E, *A History of South East Asia,* McMillan, London, 1968

Halliday, Fred, "Students of the World Unite", Cockburn, Alexander and Robin Blackburn, *Student Power,* Penguin, London, 1969

Kh Loken, "Student Movement in Manipur", unpublished seminar paper, presented in ICSSR-Political Science Deptt., MU in 1990

Lasswell, Harold, *Psychopathology and Politics,* University of Chicago Press, 1930

Levy, Marion J, Jr. *Modernization and The Structure of Societies,* Princeton University Press, New Jersey, 1966

Lexicon Universal Enclyclopedia

Lipset, Syemour M,(ed), *Student Politics,* Basic Books, New York, 1967

Lipset, Seymour M, "Students and Politics in Comparative Perspective" in P G Altbach, *The Student Revolution: a Global Analysis,* Lalvani, Bombay, 1970

M C Arun, "Constitutional History of AMSU" in *Regional Integration,* vol XVII-XIX, Imphal

Mansukhani, G S, *Student Power in India,* Oxford-IBH, New Delhi, 1975

Mitra, A, *Report on Inquiry of Police Firing at Imphal on 27-8-1965,* Manipur Legislative Assembly, Imphal, 1968

Nagel, Julian (ed), *Student Power,* Merlin Press, London, 1969

Naorem Sanajaoba, ed., *Manipur: Past and Present, Vol. I,* Mittal Publication, New Delhi

Paloczi-Horath, George, *Youth Up In Arms,* Weidenfeld and Nicolson, London, 1971

Ross, AD, *Student Unrest in India: A Comparative Approach,* Queen's University Press, Montreal, 1969

Silverstein, Joself, "Burmese Student Politics in a Changing Society" in Philip G Altbach, *The Student Revolution: a Global Analysis,* Lalvani, Bombay, 1970

Smelser, Neil, *Theory of Collective Behavior,* Glencoe, Ill., 1963

Vajpayi, J N, *The Extremist Movement in India,* Chugh Publication, Allahabad, 1974

W Ibohal Singh, *History of Manipur,* Imphal, 1986

APPENDICES

CONSTITUTION OF THE ALL MANIPUR STUDENTS' UNION

Preamble

We, the students of Manipur determined to unite, to co-operate, and to reaffirm faith in fundamental human rights and in coexistence and to advance progress in all the aspects of life, have resolved to unite our efforts to achieve these ends; accordingly our representatives from several academic institution from different parts of this state of Manipur, assembled at Imphal, do hereby constitute a Union to be known as the "All Manipur Students' Union"

Article I

The name of the Body shall be the "All Manipur Students' Union" (AMSU). (The word "Union" occurring at any part of this constitution shall mean AMSU.

Article II

The head quarters of AMSU shall be at Imphal, the capital of Manipur State.

Article III

Non Alliance: This constitution declares that the All Manipur Students' Union shall have no alliance with any political party/organisation and it shall stand to save the fundamental human rights, the aims and objects as laid down in this constitution.

Article IV

AIMS AND OBJECTS: The aims and objects of the All Manipur Students' Union shall be:

1. To achieve common ends through equality, fraternity and justice;
2. To protect and promote educational, social, cultural, physical, moral, intellectual and scientific advancement of the general public and the students in particular through the spirit of unity, co-operation and selfless service;
3. To advance the practical significance of human welfare on the basis of democratic ideals.

Article V

Fundamental Principles: It shall be the duty of the Union to apply these principles in executing the articles of this constitution and see that any amendment to this constitution is in conformity with these principles.

1. The Union shall devote its activities in bringing to an end to qualities among the students;
2. The Union shall strive for justice and a clean society where there is no fear for everybody due to lack of justice or otherwise;
3. The Union shall take up any programme that is deemed to be carried out at demand from time to time in conformity with the objectives of the Union.

Article VI

Membership: The Union shall have the following classes of members:

1. Founder Members: The students representative of the Institutions which participated and signed in the register of the General Assembly meeting held on the 12th September, 1965 at Imphal shall be the Founder Members of the Union.
2. Members of the General Assembly: Any bonafide representative of the educational institutions right from high school or its equivalence upto University level in Manipur which is affiliated to or recognised by AMSU shall become a member of the General Assembly.
3. Members of the Executive Council: Any member of the General Assembly, if he/she is elected as a member of the Executive Council shall automatically become a member of the Executive Council.
4. Ordinary Members: Any student of an affiliated/ recognised educational institutions shall be an ordinary member of the Union.

Article VII

The Administrative Organ of the Union: The Union shall have the following Administrative Organs, viz.,

1. General Assembly
2. Executive Council
3. District Committees and such other committees as may be formed by the Executive Council, from time to time.

Article VIII

The Administration of the Union: The General Assembly shall have the representatives from each affiliated educational institutions. Each members institution shall have only one vote.

The President of the AMSU shall preside over the meeting of the General Assembly and in his absence the Vice-President shall preside over the said meeting and if both are found absent, the General Assembly shall elect one from among the members and he/she shall preside over the meeting.

Terms, Power, Functions, Meeting, Quorum and Requisition

The General Assembly

a. It shall be the duty of the General Assembly
    1. To see that the Constitution of the Union is followed by its members/organs and take up such steps as may be necessary for the smooth implementation of the Constitution;
    2. Terms for General Assembly shall be one year;
    3. To frame rules consistent with the provisions of the Constitution and regulating all matters connected with the AMSU which shall be binding of all subordinate council/committees.

b. Meeting of the General Assembly: It shall meet at least once in a year with one month's notice. However, in emergency cases, a 10 days notice may be served for the meeting.

c. Quorum: The quorum of the General Assembly shall be one-third of its total membership.

d. Requisition Meeting: In case of exigency the General Secretary or the President shall convene a special meeting of the General Assembly with in one month of the receipt of the requisition to be signed by one-sixth of the members on roll of General Assembly.

e. Agenda of the Annual General Assembly shall consists of:

    1. Presentation of annual reports, discussion and acceptance thereof;
    2. Presentation of audited A/C, discussion and acceptance thereof;
    3. Election of office bearers of the next term;
    4. Amendment of the Constitution, if needed;
    5. Adoption of resolution(s), if needed.

Article IX

Executive Council: The administration of the Union shall be vested to an Executive Council consisting of a President, Vice-President, General Secretary, four Assistant Secretaries, Publicity and Information Secretary, Secretary-at-large, Auditor, Finance Secretary, two Joint Secretaries, and one representative from each district Committee.

Article X

Powers and Functions of the Executive Council: It shall be the duty of the Executive Council:

a. To receive and consider any proposal put forward by the members/Sub-ordinate Committee and take decisions thereof;

b. To implement the provisions of the Constitution and proposed such bye-laws subject to the approval of the General Assembly;

c. To approve any memorandum/statement of major importance affecting the main policy of the Union before it is issued;

d. To work for the accomplishment of the Aims and Objects of the Union;

e. To take disciplinary action against any member for his/her anti-Union activities;

f. The Executive Council shall have full controlling power to sanction any amount to carry out any programme taken up by the Union to fulfil the Aims and Objects of the Union;

g . The Executive Council may invite persons other than its members for consultation in its meetings;

h. The Executive Council shall prepare the agenda of the annual General assembly.

Article XI

Meeting and Quorum: The Executive Council shall meet as frequently as necessary with 7 days notice and quorum of the meeting shall be one-third of the total members of the Executive Council. The agenda of the Executive Council Meeting shall be prepared by the Secretary General, in consultation with the President. The notice of the meeting shall be issued by the Secretary General. In emergency cases President shall also issue notice for Executive Council meeting by giving 24 hours notice.

Article XII

Election of the Office Bearer and the Member of the Executive Council: The office bearers as mentioned in Art. IX except representatives from District Committees shall be directly elected by the Electoral College consisting of one representative from each member institution. The DC shall nominate one representative to the Executive Council.

Article XIII

District Committee, Its Power and Functions:

1. There shall be a District Committee of the AMSU in each Administrative District of the State of Manipur consisting of a District President, a District VP, District Secretary, a Treasurer, Information Secretary and six other members. Its term shall be one year and shall be conterminal with the term of General Assembly;
2. The members of the District Committee shall be elected by the members of the General Assembly residing in the same district from among themselves;
3. The District President, a District VP, District Secretary, a Treasurer, Information Secretary shall be elected by the members of the District Committee from among themselves;
4. The District Committee may meet as frequently as necessary and its quorum shall be one-fifth of its total memberships. On a week notice shall be served for a meeting of the District Committee;
5. The main function of the District Committee shall be to assist the Executive Council and the Union for achieving its aim and objects. It also shall perform such other duties as may be authorised by the Executive Council of the Union and shall have the right to solve internal district problems in consultation with the Executive Council;
6. It shall have the right to put forward proposals

which are in term with the aims and objects of the Union for consideration by the Executive Council meeting.

Article XIV

Terms of the Executive Council: The terms of the Executive Council shall be one year in normal circumstances. However, under extraordinary circumstances like occurrence of the natural calamities, war, non-holding of school/college elections, its term shall be extended upto such time until a fresh election is held.

Article XV

Power and Functions of the Office Bearers of AMSU:

1. President:

   a. The President shall be the Head of the Union;

   b. The President of the AMSU shall preside over all meeting of the Executive Council, General Assembly and any other meeting of the AMSU;

   c. The President shall above the power to convene joint setting of the Executive Council and District Committees or between District Committees. He/She also shall have the right to address meeting of any of the committee of the Union;

   d. The President shall have the power to nominate observer in regard to the functioning of the District Committee/Sub-committee etc.

   e. The President shall sign the cheque jointly with the Secretary General and the Finance Secretary;

   f. In case of voting tie he/she have a casting vote;

   g. The President shall determine the items of

business of the Executive Council in consultation with the Secretary General;

h. The President may dissolve a committee or Sub-committee etc. with the consent of the executive Council;

i. REMOVAL: The President shall not ordinarily be removed from his office without giving proper grounds. A two-third majority of the Executive Council of one-third majority of the General Assembly may propose the removal.

2. The Vice-President: The Vice-President shall have such powers as enjoyed by the President in the absence of the President. However, he may be assigned with such other functions as may be determined by the Executive Council from time to time. His normal duty shall be to assist the President.

3. Secretary General

a. Shall convene all meetings of the Union;

b. Shall record the minutes of the meetings;

c. Shall keep the records of the Union in safe custody ;

d. Shall conduct all correspondence and routine business of the Union;

e. Shall sign the cheque jointly with the President and Finance Secretary;

f. Shall implement the resolutions of the Executive Council;

g. Shall supervise the sub-committees and any affairs of the Union and report to the Executive Council.

4. Joint Secretary:

   a. Shall help the Secretary General in discharging his duty one of the Joint. Secretaries as nominated by the Executive Council shall act as Secretary General in the latter's absence;
   b. Shall act as Secretary General in the latter's absence;
   c. Shall exercise such other powers as assigned to him by the Executive Council from time to time.

5. Finance Secretary:

   a. Shall receive all payments in the name of the Union;
   b. Shall maintain account of the receipts and expenditures of the Union;
   c. Shall prepare annual balance sheet and statement of account which are to be laid before the annual General Assembly meeting;
   d. Shall keep a pass book of the Bank and other financial documents in safe custody;
   e. Shall sign all the cheques jointly with the President and Secretary General;
   f. Shall collect the receipt and expenditure accounts of the District Committee and shall incorporate the same in preparation of Annual Balance sheet of the Union to be presented in the Annual General Assembly meeting.

6. Publicity and Information Secretary:

   i. Shall inform the Executive Council of any matter connected with the Union in time;

ii. Shall inform the members of the Union and all the other matter as may be authorised by the Executive Council;

iii. Shall publish such matters as may be authorised by the Executive Council from to time.

7. Assistant Secretary:

a. There shall be four Assistant Secretaries, Secretary at large and shall perform the duties as assigned by the Executive Council from time to time to carry out the programme of the Union.

8. Secretary at large:

The Secretary at large shall co-ordinate between the different committee, sub-committee, sub-committee and District Committee and shall see the committees are functioning properly as satisfactorily.

9. Auditor:

The Auditor shall audit the account of the Union and Prepare the Audited Account of the Union after consultation with Finance Secretary, and he shall have independent right to audit the account of the Union under normal rules.

Article XVI

Advisory Council: There shall be an Advisory Council of the Union consisting of the Ex-Executive Council members and such other members as nominated by the Executive Council. The normal duty of the Advisory Council shall be to advise and guide the Union on the line of the Constitution. Its meetings shall be presided over by one of the advisors. The term of the Advisory Council shall be one year.

Article XVII

Mode of Fund Drive and Accounting:

i. The fund drive shall be done through a common receipt book supplied by the Executive Council of the Union;

ii. 25% of the fund raised by the District Committee shall be contributed to the common fund operated by the Executive Council;

iii. Statement of Receipt and Expenditure of the District Committee shall be submitted to the Executive Council to draw up annual balance sheet of the Union.

Article XVIII

Symbol

Article XIX

Flag: White flag with the words "Learn, Serve, Sacrifice" in semi circle and the words "All Manipur Students' Union" at the bottom of the flag in green colour. The size of the flag should be in the ration 2:3 in respect of breadth and length.

Article XX

Language of the Union: The state official language, i.e., Manipuri or English language shall be official language of the Union.

Article XXI

Amendment

Any amendment of advancement of the Constitution may be made by two-third of the General Assembly.

ANNEXURES

ANNEXURE-I

1. The Election Committee

i. There shall be an Election Committee consisting of (a) President of the Union, (b) General Secretary, (c) two members of the Executive Council to be nominated by the Executive Council, (d) three other members to be nominated by the President of the Union;

ii. The President of AMSU shall be the Chairman of the Committee shall preside all the meetings of the Election Committee and the Secretary General shall act as the Member Secretary of the Committee.

2. Returning Officer and Assistant Returning Office

The Election Committee shall appoint two of its members as Returning Officer and Assistant Returning Officer of any of the Election of the AMSU. However, in the case of Election to District Committee, the Election Committee may/shall appoint tow members of the District to act Returning Officer/Assistant Returning Officer.

3. Members of the Election Committee not to contest for any office of the Executive Council and District Committee

If any member of the Election Committee desire to contest for any office bearer of the Union, he/she shall cease to become such members and the resultant vacancy shall be filled in by such persons nominated by the Executive Council.

4. Powers and Functions

The Election Committee shall held Annual Election to Executive/District Committee.

5. Election Disputes

A candidate or his agent may submit an election petition to the Chairman of the Committee within 24 hours of the declaration of the election result and the decision of the declaration of the Election Committee to any election dispute shall be final. The Election Committee shall not take more than two months in deciding an election case.

ANNEXURE I (B)

ELECTION RULES: MODE OF ELECTION

1. Election to any office bearer of the Union shall be by secrete ballot and each member shall have one vote.

2. At least 20 days notice shall be given for election to the Executive Council/District Committees.

3. Final Electoral Rolls shall be made available to the voters at least 10 days before the date of election.

4. Presiding and Polling Officer: The Election Committee shall nominate two members of the Executive Council as Presiding and Polling Officer respectively of the election to the Executive Council. However, for the election of the District Committees, the outgoing President and the

Secretary of the District shall act as Presiding and Polling Officer respectively of the election.

5. Nomination Papers: All nomination papers shall be submitted to the Returning Officer/Assistant Returning Officer before seven days of the date of election. The proposers and seconders of the candidate shall be member of the General Assembly.

6. Election to Executive Council shall be held at Imphal, the HQ of the Union, at such place and time and date as may be fixed by the Executive Council. However, for District Committee elections may be held at suitable place in the District and preferably at the HQ of the District.

7. All affiliated/recognised institutions shall send only one representative as voter/electorate from among the members of the students' unions of the respective institution duly countersigned by the Head of the institution at least twelve days before the date of the election.

8. High School or its equivalent and institutions for Higher study shall be eligible to nominate members to the General Assembly.

9. Qualification of a candidate:

a. *Executive Council:* A candidate for any office of the Executive Council (i) shall be a member of the General Assembly, (ii) shall not be of unsound mind, (iii) shall not be a member of any political party or its students' wing;

b. *District Committees:* A candidate for any office bearer of the President and the General Secretary of the Executive Council shall, in addition to the qualifications mentioned in Rule 9 (nine) above, be students of Degree or equivalent or above.

10. Scrutiny of nomination paper: shall take place on the next day of the last date of the submission of the nomination papers. Physical presence of the candidate and proposer and seconder shall be necessary at the time of scrutiny.

11. Counting of vote:

a. A candidate may nominate any voter as counting agent to represent him at the time of counting of votes.
b. All democratic rules as prevailing in this state shall be applied for the counting of votes.
c. The Returning Officer of the Election Committee shall issue a Certificate of Election to each successful candidate as soon as the results are declared.

FORM OF OATH OR AFFIRMATION

I, ..., do swear in the name of god/ solemnly affirm that, I will bear true faith and all to the Constitution of the All Manipur Students' Union and that uphold the integrity of the students, that I will faithfully and consciously discharge my duties as for the AMSU.

INDEX

U

W

Y